THE EAST COUNTRY

The East Country

ALMANAC TALES OF VALLEY AND SHORE

JULES PRETTY

COMSTOCK PUBLISHING ASSOCIATES
a division of
CORNELL UNIVERSITY PRESS
Ithaca and London

First published 2017 by Cornell University Press

Printed in the United States of America

Library of Congress Cataloging-in-Publication Data

Names: Pretty, Jules N., author.
Title: The East Country : almanac tales of valley and shore / Jules Pretty.
Description: Ithaca : Comstock Publishing Associates, a division of Cornell University Press, 2017. | Includes bibliographical references.
Identifiers: LCCN 2017005230 (print) | LCCN 2017007395 (ebook) | ISBN 9781501709333 (pbk : alk. paper) | ISBN 9781501709357 (epub/mobi) | ISBN 9781501709340 (pdf)
Subjects: LCSH: Stour Valley (Cambridgeshire, Essex, and Suffolk, England)—Description and travel. | Country life—England—Stour Valley (Cambridgeshire, Essex, and Suffolk) | Natural history—England—Stour Valley (Cambridgeshire, Essex, and Suffolk)
Classification: LCC DA670.S77 P74 2017 (print) | LCC DA670.S77 (ebook) | DDC 942.6—dc23
LC record available at https://lccn.loc.gov/2017005230

Cornell University Press strives to use environmentally responsible suppliers and materials to the fullest extent possible in the publishing of its books. Such materials include vegetable-based, low-VOC inks and acid-free papers that are recycled, totally chlorine-free, or partly composed of nonwood fibers. For further information, visit our website at www.cornellpress.cornell.edu.

For
my mother, Susan,

and

Gill, Freya, and Theo

Last 2 nights, at dusk,

6 mature stag beetles flying in the garden. 4 males & 2 females.

A pipistrelle weaved in & out of them.

With care.

Tweet (@JulesPretty1), one 20th of June

Live in a good place
Keep your mind deep.

Lao-Tzu, Tao Te Ching

CONTENTS

Crossing the New Year   123

PREFACE

At that time, long ago, glaciers were in retreat, and meltwaters gushed eastwards. Valleys were scoured, and water exited at the new shores of Suffolk and Essex. One river, the Stour, was the boundary between counties that became famed kingdoms of Angles and Saxons. The valley was a matchless mosaic. It was painted at the silk town, Sudbury, by Gainsborough, by Constable and Munnings at the lower flats and fords, in the middle reaches by John Nash, fashioned by farmers and free-draining sandy loams. We are at the border, on the slopes of one county, in sight of the other.

The landscape is both farmed and wild, designated near fifty years for outstanding natural beauty. There are deer and bat, returned otter and rare stag beetle; fields of onion, potato, sugar beet; rippling stands of malt barley and milling wheat; dappled orchard and survivor elm; flowered cottage garden and allotment; longhorn cattle and murmuring sheep, the air hushed with the scent of honeysuckle. Overhead plane buzzards, flocks of jostling jackdaw and rook roaming and roosting together. The vale twice was menaced by dragons, short battles, and long tales, and in a hilltop chapel the country's crown was placed on a flaxen fifteen-year-old. The churches have their symbols, yet also stone beast, Green Man in roof timber, in one chapel's stained glass, the green philosopher and composer Hildegard of Bingen. The waters of the river are often crystal clear, cordate lily flowered yellow and white, spear of rush and gossamer grass, shadowy pike in the deeps. There are hidden places, cool glades in woodland, riffles over weirs, silent pools and swirling midges, track of fox, and tall alder, black poplar, bat willow, old oak. There are no mountains in this east country; just sharp hill, tapestry valley, liminal marsh, coastal cliff, mudflat and shingle beach.

"There are some who can live without wild things, and some who cannot," wrote Aldo Leopold in 1949. His desire for a land ethic was infectious. His wooden shack in Wisconsin with the white door and window frames was raised in a wasteland. Now it stands beside mature beech and pine, the tall-grass prairie swaying rich with flowers.

It might have been five minutes ago, maybe more. I sat on stumps with Aldo's daughters Nina and Estella, both in their late winters. We talked about links with the land. How these could shape the way we think and act, how food systems change, how attentiveness might rescue the planet from overconsumption. We walked by the lazy river pooling at sandbanks, and heard the clangor of crane. They clutched photographs of how the land looked when they were young. Those changes are proof alone that in wildness lies some salvation. Annie Dillard observed that wild places should not be thought of as out of the way; they should be in the way. You just need to go into them and feel. In this patchwork valley, all we see arises from choice: by family farmer, conservation body, gardener, local authority; also the developer. There is food and nature, interwoven, as they always were.

Matsuo Bashō walked far and learned to be still, nature always in and out of his short life and writing. The haiku form has an association with a particular season, provoked by a *kigo* trigger word. There seem to be fewer in English, perhaps becoming rarer as foods have become available year-round, as seasonal ceremonies have been diluted by the timeless modern. Yet strawberries are still associated with flush of summer; bonfire night with mists of autumn. What remains: barbecue signs summer heat, mulled wine only winter evenings. Nightingales sing for spring, swifts mark it with flashing flights, swallows call autumn's approach huddled on wires. The pause of spring: a cuckoo call.

We could all develop long attachments to the local. Being on the land does change us. This bricolage of tales emerged from journeys on the land and coast of the east country, echoing the ebb and flow of seas over seasons. Everything we do is influencing the world: we create the world by experiencing it. It creates us too by our experiences and discoveries. Yet there is darkness also, at the edge of dreams, between shadow and hope, always a dying and a living. It happens just as much in the dim depths of the woods, on lapping marshes, inside crumbled industrial estates hemmed by chain-link. Things are far from safe, beyond the poem, observed the wholesome magician Seamus Heaney. Yet the works might persist.

There are many signs of such permanence; others of rapid change. Estrangement from the land brings a modern loneliness. Edward Abbey said protectively in *Desert Solitaire*, "Don't go into the desert," but actually meant *do*. Robert Macfarlane wrote of J. A. Baker's Essex *Peregrine*, "Very little happens, over and over again." This is how it can be, except of course everything is happening. Plantsman-poet Stanley Kunitz observed a wild permissiveness in his mind whilst he gardened: "I learned I could go anywhere in my inner life."

"Never try to explain," he also wrote of our engagement with the wild and domestic. "The danger is that you can so tame your garden that it becomes a thing." And in so taming and developing, we lose so much. At the southern edge of Essex, D. W. Gillingham walked far fields and forests in the 1930s to write *Unto the Fields*, a book so dense with wildlife it is clear today we see only impoverishment:

"The ploughland flickered with birds, and the hedges too; there was an immense flock of chaffinches and yellow hammers, together with migrant larks, and crows and stockdoves and wood pigeons and chack-chacking fieldfares and lapwings, so much life, indeed, that I could not observe it all at once." He wrote of gatherings of tits on the forest floor rustling so loud he thought they were deer; two hundred redwing amongst the haws. Richard Jefferies wrote of similar bird abundance in his southern county: our baselines have shifted.

Out on the land of wild and garden, there does not have to be loneliness. Nothing is empty and spare: stare at the fine veins in a petal, the grain of a pebble. It should be troubling that average well-being and life satisfaction have not changed in the UK or USA since the mid-twentieth century, even though economic wealth per person has risen fourfold. We have more, we spend more, we are not happier. A painful price is being paid.

It could get worse. Elsewhere progress has brought dramatic benefits, though not to all. The gaps are growing, the good things could be lost. There will be a heavy cost to restoring a collapsed climate. Yet many trade in doubt, denying evidence as mere rumor or fiction. There are many threats to the valley. This book is not a call to action. But doubters or deniers, just stop here, throw this book away. Or give it to someone younger. It will be their world before long. You pick up a stone on a cold beach, it grows warm in the hand. It retains the warmth of life, then further along after time has passed you drop it in the shingle, and it becomes bone cold again. We will be robbed of breath soon enough.

Nature will carry on regardless. It is just that we might not.

Some conflicts are in inner space. Some solutions might just lie in the outer space, those places we gaze upon and with which we can form attachments. The explorer Robin Hanbury-Tenison said, "Journeys should have impacts that resonate through the years." They should, in short, be tales that never lose in the telling.

So. The east country is like no other place, yet it is every other place. These stories interweave several years in the valley and along the salty shore. There are twelve monthly acts to this almanac, and a spin in the scenes that binds us to nature, as it ever did.

Verse that is centered on the page is my own. Explanatory notes for most stories can be found at the end of the book, containing links to key references and further details on quotations, locations, and terminology.

A GEOGRAPHIC LOCATOR

Every place has an east country, where dawn and dusk come first. This one is in the mid-northern latitudes, neither tropic nor boreal, just a degree to the sunny side of the meridian of zero longitude. Seven to eight thousand years ago, the British Isles were connected by land to the continent, Doggerland, an expanse of wide lagoon and salt marsh, mudflat and inland stream, birch parkland and tunnel valley. Water locked up by the last ice age was released, no one could stop the rising tide, and Britain and Ireland were surrounded by salty seas. At the far east, rivers now flowed into the North Sea. Look at a map, find the semicircle north of England's capital, London. Or find the low countries on Europe's western shore, and sail west. There you will find this east country. Every place has one, where big questions are partially hidden, lost in landscape, nature, and words, inside months and seasons too. Slow down, take time, live local, keep your mind deep. Here is one east country. There are many others, where everything is in fact paradise.

THE EAST COUNTRY

JANUARY

1. THE WINTER HESITATION

Ah. Long ago, winter was dark and always cold.

These days the east country sighed silence. There was not a natural sound. A neighbor's boiler leaked a condensation cloud, a blinking plane gassed high above. There were neither dogs nor barking deer. The birds had flown, or were dead. Jupiter was bright on the dome of night sky. By Cassiopeia flowed two shooting stars, a streak of silver, a short golden tear of the fabric. Underfoot crunched frozen snow. The raw night heaved hard, beating at walls.

It had been warm. In new terra-cotta, four Japanese maples were potted. Months will pass before they leaf. The clutter by shed and oil tank was now neat, all the while the slow black rooks cawing and spinning on the gray canvas of cloud. Down here songbirds were winning territories, yet it was not spring. In afternoon dusk, there were branches of apple and pear to prune. From the saw and the sweat, logs appeared. It was a simple business. They will season a year. It was much work for a modest pile. At the far end of the garden, a spotted woodpecker thrummed. Still there was a hesitation on the land.

It was a time for calling. At Ronald Blythe's, upriver on the Wormingford side, we talked over tea. The cat shed white hair, the yeoman's house creaking in the cold. It will be Benjamin Britten's one-hundredth anniversary: Ronnie had written of his time by the sea. It will be the coastal floods' sixtieth too, at the end of the month. As another dreaming darkness fell, we came to talk of poet laureates of the past, and Ronnie handed on a tall walking stick made and given by John Masefield. At home, somewhere on shelves was "Sea Fever" and rhythms of lonely sea and sky, ways long passed and much forgotten.

Across oceans, Australia burned, trees flaming under scalding skies. Here pressure dropped, winter gathered up, winds rushed from afar. There were atmospheric roars of disapproval. Shrub and tree shook and took fright. Low cloud departed, the mercury fell to minus 10 °C. The sun rose into a blinding blue sky, the land briefly bright. Silent cold froze small birds, encouraged cats, soured dreams. On the farms, it was days for ditching and hedging; in former times for cutting reed and catching pike and eel.

The Christmas tree had been stripped of decoration. It was discarded, its time was over. The honeysuckle sprouted tiny leaves, the lawn gone to moss. The kids were back in London, out much with friends. From deep in the country, you easily forget the city appeal.

A reminder: winter is winter, not the beginning or end, it happens every year. Yet in the grip of cold, still the gaze is drawn upward, the dream for longer days and laughing in the sun. More snow fell, strangely from the south. Plant pots were rimed with white. Still the emails kept coming, though the fields were icy and roads impassable.

> And all I ask is a merry yarn from a laughing fellow-rover
> And quiet sleep and a sweet dream when the long trick's over.
> John Masefield, 1878–1967

—————

2. ONE GLOSSY IBIS AND MANY TICKS

Out on the salt marsh was a tropical bird.

The glossy ibis was on the scrape, probing pools with curved bill. The flood tide swallowed sinuous creeks, rising so far that Geedon was gone under glassy miles of sky. The burgundy bird fed on. A flock of avocet glittered on cold Colne River, disappearing as they shivered, whirling white over ranked shield duck. On two marsh posts were hard-eyed peregrine. There will be panic and plucking, before long.

> Far away at Mersea Island,
> Where a marsh rector wrote of wetland drama,
> A yacht swung at anchor,
> Facing now the curling current.
> In minutes marsh grass and sea lavender reappeared.
> Such tidings:
> Winter ibis, avocet back, the tide on the ebb,
> The economy in debt.

Not long ago, locals looked on muck and marsh as a larder, even as mosquito bit. All was eaten, winkle and oyster, rabbit and deer, samphire pickled, flounder found by barefoot children, mushroom from the flats. In modern times, such hunting and gathering has almost gone, ruined by cheap chicken; then recession sparked a poaching revival. In those days, birds were snagged in herring nets staked on slick mud: in the pot went *kittie*-black-headed gull, *harnser*-herring gull, *tewkie*-redshank, *greenie*-greenshank, *arcty* tern. City collectors bought rarities, and a century ago up at Breydon Water, Arthur Patterson recorded spoonbill, avocet, osprey, buzzard, and white-tailed eagle. After clamming his outland shore with feet ached and abraded, Robert Finch wrote, the "hunter is preferable to the developer."

But there long had been another threat: the swamp ague was in these eastern marshes also to a century ago, the people of Essex and Suffolk scrapping to survive malaria. Pub landlords laced beer with opium bled from yellow-horned poppy. In the 1500s, John Norden called it a "most cruel quartene fever"; on his grand tour of the 1720s, Daniel Defoe heard tell of marsh farmers taking ten to fifteen inland wives a lifetime, the farmworkers laughing into their beer as they spun tall tales. There was a grain of truth. It was kill or cure country, down on the salt. For no known reason, the plasmodium ague then was gone.

Eel was a staple for the wetland east, then it too quit. South to London, they were jellied, baked with thyme and onion, dosed with vinegar. Elvers pitch up in March, three years as larvae then as glass eels migrating from the far Sargasso Sea. In muds and meres, they lay low for twenty years, as adults drawn back over dry land on moonless winter night. Eel were caught as they left for the sea; elver on arrival. Years ago, a village boy held one, fat as a blacksmith's arm, up on Abel's Bridge, his thin arms outstretched for all to see. The brick bridge was funded by a clothier in the Tudor wool boom: the village was Britain's forty-fifth-largest settlement in those times. Eels, though, were abundant then not.

In the 1950s, Ambrose Waller wrote of the Stour, "Common eel is everywhere, the elvers climbing up floodgates in spring." Now near-extinction has plunged populations to one hundredth in twenty years. Again, a mystery: rivers straightened, dredged, and drained, plastic pollution, overfishing, a parasite, something odd in ocean currents. Worse than not knowing why is who is at fault. Is this a fatal decline, has it happened before?

The shadowed grass glistened, a salmon sun latched on the low western sky. In winter's lonely marsh one foot was always wet and the other dry, yet this was only fifty miles from the safe metropolis. Now another sign of ecological ebb and flow. Ticks are active in warm months, now surviving these tepid winters. Wherever go sheep or deer, Lyme disease feeds fear. From damp vegetation, ticks leap for legs. The signs: a rash for weeks, growing to bull's-eye, then flu, joint pain, nerve inflammation. It's boots for hunter, fisher, birdwatcher, and walker.

3. WINTER GALES AND BELIEFS

The inventive landscape of dark dreams was set to stalk that year. A midwinter gale shrieked on land and sea. Trees failed to flee the methodical violence, sprang back, were lashed again. Many went down, blocking ways. In the west and north it was the worst for years. Big seas, no electricity, a menace to more than daily plans. It had been a genial winter, until then, of light winds and squally rain. The previous year we had been stranded by a month of snow, sledging at the airfield on the hill. Not this year. The last was the second-warmest on record; East Anglia had the second-driest ever; Scotland the wettest. Yet birds had sensed the passing of the solstice: they were singing for spring. In the garden, a forsythia had three flowers; it was thinking of March. The lilac was leafing out; it guessed April. Two roses flowered yesterday, a yellow and a marble white.

Can the evidence make any difference? A hot dry year down here; wet up north. Each year, carbon dioxide in the atmosphere increases by two parts per million and now has passed 400. In preindustrial times it was 280; to protect the planet from disruption we need it back at 350. But such a return is improbable, given converging consumption patterns and worldwide appetite for energy-intensive economies. It will be hard to stop at 450, even if leaders in affluent countries get the message. Bird, insect, and plant are marching north and up. Each decade ranges are racing at the poles by six kilometers, in elevation by six meters. But here is the problem: numbers seem to work only for those disposed to believe. Most of us want stories of hope, not doom. How tempting to look away. In the end, all will be victims. This one boat will founder, many go down.

In *Ecologies of the Heart*, Eugene Anderson observed: "No previous culture has ever known so much about the environment. No civilization has ever managed the environment more carelessly." In appealing to the rational, we also need ritual and ceremony to fix new beliefs and codes of behavior, to tie us to the land, to make it matter more. New taboos would be good, as well as new incentives. Landscapes can contain deep emotion; we need attachment, by whatever means.

"It doesn't matter about the beliefs," wrote Anderson, "what matters is the end."

How then to garnish nature with the desire to care? Yesterday the garden was wind-battered. Hailstones piled high on bubble-wrapped pots. By day, small birds hunkered down, rook and jackdaw flying high. They gathered up in corvid crowds, twisting and tumbling, accelerating fast downwind, beating back up. They seemed to be enjoying themselves. In *The Abstract Wild*, Jack Turner recorded this: at an air base north of San Francisco, gulls flew into the turbulent blast of jet engines on R-316 bombers: "They would simply disappear, only to turn up a few seconds later a quarter of a mile downwind, apparently having enjoyed the experience as much as a child running through a hose—even coming around eager-eyed for more."

It had been just before Christmas. On the raised river wall the sun set inland and dusk fell. Up at Southwold, my father was better after seemingly terminal stays at two hospitals. A harried nurse whipped a sticky plaster off his papery arm, a bloody tear of rectangular skin. All gasped: he was home that day. The tide ebbed, curlew burbled on the cold mudflat, knot jumped at the water's edge, gulls cried. In winter, sorrow stalks the land, awaiting dispatch. Yet that day, many people were walking, connecting with a little bit of wild as the sun shimmered low. Most of us own cameras; that day, more sunset images were added to the celebratory record, all statements: we were there.

<hr />

4. WALK THE LINE

The river Alde rises in farmland and flowed to meet the sea at foggy Aldeburgh. From the Middle Ages, longshore drift and tides that flood south scoured up shingle and swamped the river mouth. Now the spit is twelve miles long, the shape-shifting river starting with one name and ending with another, tumbling out as the Ore at Shingle Street. It was before dawn, the eastern sky lilac, the shadows fraught with frost.

At first, all was familiar. Pastel cottage, rusting capstan, bank of shingle, the first purple sprout of sea kale, shingle-blanched stems once a favored food. Water architects had been at work. The river mouth had moved, gouging out a bay and new island. At the shore was now a steep levee, six meters high. Fresh water poured into the steely sea, jostling up a wall of rapids. It was low tide, the southeast wind dashing wave on stone. There was not long to wait: the sun leapt from the sea, it was warmer. The light glittered gold on the waves. A long shadow cast inland, there was simply sea and stone, a crush and rush, suck and pull, thrown back again. From the wall of shingle, fresh springs bubbled down to the sea. When William Dutt passed this way in the early 1900s, the Ore mouth was north at Hollesley Bay.

Some miles south were war emplacements at Bawdsey, but first the white line. A few years back, twenty thousand limey whelk shells were laid out as land art. The line was elastic linking cottage to the sea, and had eroded, sunk into the toffee shingle, diminished, wobbled, but still survived. It was a short walk, two hundred meters up one side, past circles and helices, replacing shells knocked to one side, back down the other, doing the same. The winter sun blazed on the twenty-four coast guard windows, exploded off the old schoolhouse.

Eyes down and open: there were stones with holes and the holes filled with smaller stones—one black, one tan, one white. Then the unique glamour of an old dragon's underground vault long-grassed over: a piece of amber, glowing gold and lit from within. There was a rectangle of bottle-green glass, the sun shining through this prism too.

Stone, amber, glass:
Made by earth, made by tree, made by human.
The winter morning lit them all.

It was a six-mile walk to advance two. The Suffolk shingle mile has always been a long one. A line of wet steps stretched the way, where rock of granite riprap protected the ness with its Martello tower, put up to see off Napoleon. Bawdsey lost its pub in the 1970s and shop in the next decade, not to the sea, but to the economy. Inland was an observation tower by flooded pool and scolding coot. Ironwork on the upper gallery said in beaded metal: *Prisoner of War*. The artist had sprayed war words inside: *Friend or Foe*, *Flying under the Radar*, *Riding the Waves*. Access was limited: the basement flooded, iron ladder to the upper stories severed. For centuries, on and off, defenders of these islands have looked east and waited. Others told stories: nearby did FitzGerald translate the *Rubaiyat*.

On return, the tall seawall was muddy yet solid. A crow flew to a post, crossed to the next, calling on. Skylark elevated from grassy meadow on the back shingle. A male and female stonechat perched at a bramble thicket, dipped behind. Inland, on a field of cultivated kale were fifty whooper swan. Juveniles were still in gray, some adult pairs stood alone. On the salt-side, restless redshank pinked warning. When fog descends, the green buoy booms to sea, one of sixty-two once tethered to shifting sands and swatchways of Cork Ledge and Cork Knock, Cutter Sands, Kettle Bottom, Ridge and Gabbard, Slipwest too.

After a talk to Snape Women's Institute in the autumn, a local woman said of Shingle Street she loathed the melancholy. There was *An Incident* in the war, bodies washed in waves, the sea aflame, all hushed up. No one knows if they were British, American, or German, whether it was accident, dreadful experiment, or great success: rumor of repulsed invasion would raise domestic morale. When the secret papers were released, acute disappointment: the mysteries remained, the text redacted. Another WI member said her uncle was transferred to Shingle Street from Leiston radiator factory. They needed his plumbing skills: he told her there was a secret network of pipes filled with flammable liquid. Earlier, on the shore, war remnants were exposed at low tide, concrete shapes made with shingle and little lime. Myths are made by cover-ups.

At one cottage a fiery collie barked and banged at a fence. On the ground was a bleached bird bone, a moonstone crusted with orange lichen. Inland, a military helicopter thropped over the remote prison, location too of rare Suffolk Punch herd. It slipped to pine woodland, searching still. There was more work to do, walking back along the line. In a West Coast jail, Johnny Cash sang:

I keep a close watch on this heart of mine
I keep my eyes wide open all the time
. . . I walk the line.

Johnny Cash, 1932–2003

---

5. THE WEIGHT OF A SNIPE

A charm of thirty goldfinch was in the silver birch.
Twittering and wheezing, looking to the feeders.
The air was cold,
Migrating into lungs then burning hot.

The days lengthen slowly, a month after the solstice. Sunrise will shift ten minutes over the next ten days, sunset by sixteen. Still no snow, wet underfoot, the sky on the valley floor. Over the garden, rooks slid across the sky.

Still. The atmosphere had fled. The skeletons of trees were unmoving. The air was chilled, plumes of breath above the mossy lawn that quick crunched below. The moon was bright to the southeast, to the south Jupiter and Orion shining too, the other stars bleached away. On the grassy ground were shadows of trees, branches, branchlets. A smear of silver moonlight, guinea fowl creaking up the hill. All else had stopped. The raw air gripped at bare feet. Winter now was this night of cold and the world had come to a halt. Fronts charged in, but not here. Rain approached, but not yet here.

Seamus Heaney said a friend thought the human soul was about the weight of a snipe. It is a small bird, given to tremulous drumming. We dwell here, but also in the memory. Then lie weightless in a box.

The sign that things might change was a patch of blue in mist on the hilltop. Inside the cloud the land was small. Wet roads, beads of a thousand droplets on grass panicles, no sound of skylark, the sun too low. The narrow lanes were madly busy, drivers gripping wheels on full gas, none giving way. It was a sign. There was debris in the gutter, racing water in roadside ditch, then a lane itself a raging river. These back ways were normally quiet: oddly more drivers dueled.

On a road under a hill where dragons clashed, a vehicle was on its roof. The hedge bank had been plowed deep, the sporty car with the soft top and now no top flipped and spun to block the way. Three people were standing: one had been reckless. The police had been called, declared the man. Two women looked stunned, perhaps not by accident but at survival. The land continued gurgling, water racing from every drain. The road was stilled. Cars queued in both directions.

More rain was due.
Snowdrops were bright and cow parsley a hand high.
In flower were golden gorse and dead nettle.

And so, as the light bled from the sky, the power quivered off, television shuddering and the wind rushing on. Flash on horizon, the house darkened. The storm dashed in, crashing over all the land, pushing a wall of rain. The trees tore up, the lightning purple-blue on the dome of the sky, each flash followed by deeper dark. It seemed the beginning of an apocalypse. Later the lights flickered back on. It will have been the wettest January ever.

—⟨⟨⟨ ⟩⟩⟩—

6. THE OLD BATTLEFIELD

Across the dark mud lay Northey Island. On this side the dizziness of the battlefield. The rattling gale poured from west, the lane turning tight between gray houses, through a farmyard and down to the shore. In the year 991 here lined up Essex Saxons under tall Byrhtnoth, bright-courage, across the wet causeway Olaf and his ninety-three longships. The poet wrote of the Battle of Mealdune, England's treasure town on the hill, a singular saga by the saltiest river. Would the land taint those tales?

Ahead a tractor clattered, pulling up staves of iron where repairs to under-mud cables had failed. We pulled up zips, tightened straps, walked to the seawall. On the shore side the battlefield was a crop of kale a couple of meters up from marsh. All around would have been salty creeks and smooth sweet mud. The sun rose above the Dengie into a slit of golden sky. Clouds dashed past. Light glinted on the town to the west. In those days, the inhabitants prepared to watch deadly sport, fearful in the stands. Tall dragon prows and square sails, the vindictive fleet pulled up so visible. Heard the ringing of iron on shields: raid the mint, pay the Danegeld, and we will sail away. The white-haired earldorman was not for paying. He oft had seen the Vikings come for more. But in the courts, the clever king held the throne by paying, using other people's money.

Light blazed on mudflat, the tide at its lowest. The causeway curved left and then right to form an arc. Ahead was grassy slope and thicket of thorn. Long shadows stretched from clumps of bladder wrack.

Redshank flitted, crying,
Had done for a thousand years.
A barge lay stranded in the channel.
A flock of knot went up,
Flickered out and in,
Descended again.

Here was a perfect beach for ships, the fleet massive. They could have moored for a quick escape on the far side, but visibility was their play. This was the greatest invasion force, the locals should know. A promontory faced the mud and town: here the king's fire was lit and he stood and waited, listening, the chuckle of tide, watching, birds in thousands twisting and turning as falcons stooped from high.

It was wet underfoot, slate-gray sky above. A path turned along the seawall, the land bright green on the inside and olive on the salty. The sloping meadow was poached by cattle, yet was a vantage point where the Vikings stood in lines and faced the shoremen. In the poem, Wulfstan and two brave men stood on the causeway and held back the horde. A fiction: they would have been run over. The invitation was accepted and the Vikings crossed to fight, a choreographed sport with a start time and no referee.

Inland a flock of geese gabbled, a tumbled crowd of speckled starlings thrashing and pouring over one another. At Maldon, the sun shone on the promenade café. It was warm, the wind deflected. Rust-red mast spars of barge were tall golden patterns on the transom. Lanyards plinked, lapwings flickered. In the distance was Northey. The victorious Vikings were paid to sail, yet in twenty-five years Cnut was back to win the country's crown. He was no fool, the waves did not retreat. Such humility would be wise today.

FEBRUARY

7. PATHS AND PRINTS IN SNOW

In the beginning, static air from cold Arctic collided with a wet west front. Snowflakes fell heavily. Late evening, wind blew and sky cleared. By morning, cloud had returned, eight inches of snow and a great silence lying on the land. Such peace is a fragile thing. On with coat and hat, tighten boots, lock back door, and away to walk the muffled hills.

The snow was signed. Deer slots delicately picked across the lawn. Then rabbit, scuffling along; brown hare, hind feet together, moving at pace, two meters from one print to the next. A trail of lawless fox paws. At the Pest House, where long ago bubonic villagers were abandoned, a deer had walked through barbed wire. There were angels, blackbird-flapped wing displays. At Bugg's timber yard, guinea fowl shivered on old oak, Fred out with snow plow, doing the back roads. In the distance, the truck beeped as it reversed, moved on, pushed more snow. All else was quiet, the still air locked inside the valley.

The light was subtle, the hues narrow. It was not at all the acute intensity of the high Himalayas nor that light of the most luminous of dreams. In both, mountains sail on cobalt skies; this day the cold cloud enclosed all in a chilled blanket. Near the hilltop came a clamor of corvids: rooks chattered, jackdaws jabbered. It was a great gathering, the valley flocks attached to bare oak over sandy-brown maize. There were one thousand birds, maybe two, of jet black and gray, all in social song and symphony. It was the first snow of winter, much to tell the youngsters. They rose and tumbled, resettled to trees, to paths, to wide fields. Years ago, there was a summer rook parliament in the garden, a flock in a tree facing inward, a pair of glum birds at the center upon whom rook chatter was focused. At that time, an incomer up the valley took his gun to the noisy rookery long established in his trees. Only one should have gone, but he stayed and the birds did not.

A path dipped down a lane worn beneath fields by determined drovers and pilgrims bringing gossip. All the while birds narrated an aerial view of a cold hard land, its dark trees and distant blue remembered hills. In a haze of falling flakes were tracks of quad bike, the shepherd out early to check his sheep.

> A badger sett dug in acid soil,
> The sober snow untouched:
> They dreamed on.
> A green woodpecker arched across the meadow,
> Laughing.
> Between the wrenched land and whiten cloud,
> A hawk fast flew to a frozen branch.

In the village, small children were hauling sledges, bouncing with excitement, calling to parents; others shoveled drives, tight-lipped. A track center street had been churned clear by tires; vehicles were deep in drifts. At home, the woodstove soon filled the house with sweet resin.

There is an element of staying put and venturing forth to place-making, whatever the weather. In the garden small birds were balls of feather, possibly thirsty. The birdbaths were solid ice. The bowl of one crumbled and shattered when warmed, the composite material gone to pieces. A corner held some water, then froze. This spring and summer, the base was abandoned amongst the pots and roses, doing little. "One heavy fall of snow," wrote John Stewart Collins in *The Wood*, "and modern civilisation is silenced."

Next morning, twice the car was ice-stranded: tracks frozen until the thaw. Even with the fewest days, February can be the longest month. The depths derailed this wintertime.

Wearing flip-flops, walk in snow, carrying out the recycling. How cold it was.

> Both field and mountain
> All taken by the snow
> Till nothing remains.
> Naitō Jōshō, 1661–1704

---

8. CLOSING TIME

Sunshine streamed through curtains, light frost on flat roof. In the valley, there was a relentless wall of cold northwesterly wind. Winter grasses bent and bobbed.

All puddles were frozen, cubes of ice torn out by tires. Banks of snowdrop were the only flowers to have survived the Arctic air. Woods were dark and brooding on the horizon, yet great tits were insistent. Two chestnut cart horses lumbered across a field in search of company. Farmyards were quiet, barn doors locked. On the northern clay, hedgerows had been flailed, branchlets stripped from branches, the bark of old oaks torn. The green curtain of spring will hide much, but not for months. Whole fields of winter wheat were yellowed by frost. Fifty wood pigeons lifted from young rape, gliding into the cold vegetation. All again was silent.

There was a concrete floor by wheat on Sherbourne Street. Here for years had been an empty farm cottage, the garden tumbled with bramble and ivy, the roof back broken and all subsiding slowly. It had been harvested. There were piles of rubble, large pieces, cracked brick and soil, many cockleshells far from the sea. Tall grasses surrounded the site, would invade further. Soon no one will remember the daily drama of poverty and hopes of those who dwelled here. It has no mark on the map.

Two people were dressed smartly, one with silk headscarf, the other a cravat, walking stiffly towards a remote church; then three with dog were walking away. They nodded. In Boxford high street, most shop fronts were now private houses. The advance of progress has punched a hole. Once there was malting, brewery, watermill, and windmill, cobbler and watchmaker, three butchers, two bakers, a radio shop, general store and post office, grocer, haberdashery and dairy. There was also blacksmith, wheelwright, brickyard, carpenter, undertaker, fire station. Each had men and women with crafty skills, knowledge to cradle wood and water, metal and meat, fruit and flour, leather and fire. Today was closing time at the church, and there was chaos. Cars had pulled over on pavement, others unwilling to give way. Some chuntered past, wing mirrors snicking. Hands were waved. It was safer to wait. It must have been some sermon.

It might have been a day for being inside rather than out. Yet circular routes are more about being than arriving. Each descent is matched by climb, every tailwind by headwind, each shadow by sunlight. Now the woodstove was lit, flaming heat into the sun-washed room. In Japan, a pillow of grasses signifies being on a journey, the grass cut and folded for absorbing dreams.

To the west was watery brightness. It had been a February day like this. At the village airfield, shiny leather sofas sprouted kapok padding in the mess, the radio crackling code and location. Chairs had been carried outside. Chipped mugs held warm tea. An acrobatic biplane stalled and spun, the old engineers murmuring admiration. Suddenly the birds of hedgerow and meadow fell silent. All talk stopped. A single pigeon dashed across the airfield. With gasping violence a peregrine stooped and tierced, the prey a sudden spray of feathers and dust. Before long, song began, the purple plane looped, all breathed once more.

A lifelong friend, Kevin, was on tour from San Francisco. There was one other person in the pub. The log fire smoldered. We hunched around beers from this coast, talked of walks in the desert, of life in the Pacific city of fog and sun. And supported sports teams, the receding seasons of hope. And of the pub: bought by new developers over the hill. They have grand designs: modernize some of this dreary area, outstanding natural beauty or not. We did not need to stay to closing time.

My mother emailed a photo of my father at Fondespierre, smiling with a cold glass of rosé. Beyond was garrigue and olive grove. It made me happy and very sad.

> The summer grasses
> As if the warriors were a dream.
> Matsuo Bashō, 1644–1694

---

9. TO IKEN

Snow and ice melted. A winter week of warm daytime, a front forecast from the west. Afternoon rain was due. It was festival time: a gathering at Snape Maltings for *Place: Taking the Waters*. In the brick hall and corridors were the embattled several hundred, straightening hair and wind-tugged clothes. There were greetings in the green room. It was an exploration of the warp of water, the coast's liminal zones, a frog's-eye view from in water, how imagination unexpectedly emerges from the land. Rob Macfarlane steered the late Roger Deakin through an inland archipelago of pond and drain, there was my luminous coast, Ken Worpole reimagined estuary Essex on a national stage, Jay Griffiths weaved the weft of wild into children's lives, David Rothenberg put clarinet to Svalbard's slushy waves and the song of humpback whale.

The reed beds whispered, and Rob and I looked at the sky and decided to walk downriver to Iken. It was gray with heavy nimbostratus, spitting lightly, but not more. Wagtail bounced on the mown grass by Barbara Hepworth's *Family*, above jackdaw tumbled, the path worn around *Perceval*, the horse and cart with concrete marrows. For decades, barges sailed to land barley and refill with Garrett's malted mash for London brewers. Then came music and song.

> The row of salt-kilt oaks was upright driftwood,
> Bleached and skinned.
> Acres of sandy reeds bobbed.
> By match-poplar plantation was a harrowed field,
> A perfume rich and reeked of wet earth.
> The tide was out,
> The glistening river murmuring in and out of miles of mud.
> Curlew called.
> Overhead lazed lapwing,
> Light rain faint fell.

Wooden quays wrapped in chicken wire wandered over slick mud banks. Two Thames barges were stranded, facing downriver. The water was fresh, but twice a day the sea surges up the Ore and into the Alde Estuary, left around Iken to bring the salt. This coast was miles inland as the crow flies; even more by playful jackdaw. Half-term holidaymakers walked, one family smiling, another dragging drenched children, staring hard ahead.

A small hunter cradled a crossbow. The boy's mother stopped and said, "Did you see the seal?"

On Iken hill was St. Botolph's, the monastery cliffs meters high, the sands burrowed by badgers. There were carpets of dripping snowdrop. The bark of one craggy oak, roots eroded clear of soil, had soaked up barbed wire. Years before I lay in a punt low in the reeds, cold on the far side, the sky cloudless, the sun a stone dropping by the silhouetted church. We could hear, that day, sounds from afar, the laugh of child, clink of glass, whirr of wings, the great clanging silence of the heavens. Today, mud oozed and rain pattered on salty leaves of sea lavender.

Back inland was the young seal, creamy white. It arched on a mud bank, flopped down. By a fence post was a black-tailed godwit, hollowed by hawk or harrier. It had black-and-white wings, long beak, beauty formed and now dead and gone from this world.

At the sculptures, the sky doors slid wide. Rain sheeted down. Between the malting buildings the street was a river itself. Our faces were red and raw.

We had, it seemed, taken the waters.

—◦◦◦—

10. SATURATION

Saturation sadness. Winter bleaches the best intentions. It makes us crave for sonic spring. Let us also speak of sunshine. Cold came a North Atlantic westerly. Colors had become richer, pushing through winter gray and pale green. Under hedgerow, clumps of fresh cow parsley had appeared, months yet from shaking stands of lace. Early bluebell were glossy on a south-facing lane. A polished rook croaked from a meadow. Bramble were splattered with magnesium guano, fresh fans of vivid orange sand excavated from badger deeps. By a crumbled farm wall were blowsy daffodils, translucent yellow, citrine pale, also dark topaz. It was another sign of spring.

These days, there are few expanses of wild daffodils that might "flash upon the inward eyes," as Wordsworth wished of Cumbrian natives. Just this row, the wall danger-topped by asbestos, as are many farm buildings. There are eight thousand cultivated varieties of daffodil and narcissus. What happened to those golden hosts? It was not picking, it is written; they just went away. St. David's Day has become a celebration with daffodil, named after monk St. Dewi. Soon will be St. Winwaloe's, a Breton popular in Cornwall and East Anglia, a man of storms. March comes in like a lion, they say, and goes out like a lamb. Either way, it was dry.

On both sides of lark alley, skylark hovered and streamed their melody, jostling for territory. They look down on blocks of claimed land, saturating each with song. At the hilltop meadow, black-faced sheep bleated by bales of hay, far below the river winding blue with sky towards the new pump station. It will suck river water from Wormingford to Abberton reservoir, then on south through all of dry Essex. Only these counties in the east have escaped drought orders, reminders of those rural lives defined by springs and wells, children's work to fetch water, often miles away. In the parklands by Assington church was branch and brash of felled horse chestnut, old and partially hollowed. But flinch and weep: there would be worse. The chainsaw was ready to clear many more.

In the garden, mauve buttons of heather blurred with bees, scrambled buzzing in the mild sun. Over the lawn, motes of midge quivered. Now the tops of terra-cotta pots bubble-wrapped could be opened. Some buds were fit to burst.

By evening, the new moon was dropping in the west. There were shadows on the silvered lawn and the land had turned cold. No spring signal of barking fox. The brightest planets, Venus and Jupiter, shone like fresh beacons.

—⟞⟨⟩⟞—

11. THE BOX VALLEY

The birds knew.
Constant song inside cornflower sky.
Spring had woken.

The car was in repair at the hilltop garage, so time to walk: north down Scotland Street towards the Box Valley forty meters below. In hedgerow were arum lily, now a hand span high, varnished green, and flowing downslope chandeliers of snowdrop, pure white light beneath the rare bright sky. The white bells trembled. Rising up was feathery cow parsley. Down the narrow lane were houses of every species, thatched, Georgian, postwar, modern, up tight against the road, set back by glade and pond. A lilac cottage was for sale, a connected jungle of sheds crammed in the garden.

At the river, the route turned northwest upstream. It was three degrees, the puddles ice. Two dogs at the farm crashed into outdoor cages, the hens on the straw unmoved. A cock crowed, the dogs barked more. The path had been scarred deep by large wheels, the ruts frozen. Small were the patches of untouched grass. Cold comfort followed the river course, pile of rubble, toothed machine rusting to soil, pens of hens, one foxhole in a hillock of waste. Overlooking the flood full of sky and frozen out on the meadows were hazel bushes bright with yellow catkin. On bricks were piles of rabbit pellets. A tanker was skewed upslope, corvids rising from bare hilltop oaks.

At a large pen enclosing hollow and mound, tires for play, five pigs ran, one with black blotches, attending to the electric fence and no further. Their eyes blinked and lungs wheezed. Each had combs of white eyelashes. They were good pigs, broad in the back. The sun brightly shone in the hairs of pointed ears. It was long believed that pigs could see the wind, even rustle one up. They strolled then had to stop. They stared. Ahead was Polstead Bridge, the pigs could not come. The path was carpet bombed with molehills, between were slots of distant deer. On the hill was the old rectory, so ghosted a new vicar lasted only days. Polstead is the place of pools, celebrated not for the Red Barn murder of a mole catcher's daughter, but that her mother dreamed beyond the misdirection, Maria Marten's body being found under barn floor. At Liverpool dock, the squire's son was intercepted.

Now the light was bright, the air cold and quite still. Opposite the mill's walled garden and Kew-style glasshouse, the path stepped to a field plowed upslope.

The sun was warm and low, glimmering on the icy furrows,
Lines of water and ice on the claggy clay.
The land was wide,
Intensely lit from one hill to the other.
Midges danced above ice clear as glass,
Cracked through and melted at the edges,
Becoming water.
Beneath a giant hogweed the sky was captured in its broad umbel.

Ahead was Steps Farm, settled buildings half-abandoned, half in use at best. There was moss on asbestos roof and concrete walls painted the ochre of the farmhouse itself. A crop of bramble twisted past window frame, the green paint flaked and white base bleeding through. Two dogs yelped. The water poured off the farmyard and down drain and into ditch, feeding the Box and Stour, soon the North Sea. Yet above this hanging valley crumbled into land with its own scatter of expired machines was a row of rare black poplar, their huge branches flung at angles.

A pair of buzzards glided high, turning circles far above the corvid colony. The Open Road secondhand bookshop was open. Owner-poet Dave Charleston recommended Philip Connors's book on the lonely life of fire lookouts in the scorched Southwest, and we talked of books and families, of deaths too, still raw in all our lives. We observed approaching winters, after which there is no spring.

Next day came snow.

MARCH

12. DISTURBING HINTS OF SPRING

A long time ago, many a journey was a kind of pilgrimage. It was not just about the sacred mountain, but about being in each place along the way. The arrival at the end would be the end. The wind would roar, rain fall, the buds become a little greener. Govinda wrote, "There is no more need for any armour." Add a stone to the cairns stacked by those who passed by too.

The days grew longer. One morning the sky flared molten lava, the low clouds streaked and prominent, drawing the eye, inviting travel. Dawn lit the valley with the limitless blue of hope. The river surged higher, the fields drenched and undrained. There was lightness on the land.

More rain was due.

The body changes on a long journey. Hunger, feeling the cold, desire for comfort given up. Itch and insect bite, bruise and aching joint. Sometimes feet are blistered, each step painful. Yet one step follows another.

> Wind tore in.
> Rain was wrought from air,
> Water spilled from rivers.
> The Somerset levels were flooded,
> For weeks.
> Storms crushed the coast,
> A railway line washed away.

The house was cold and quite dark on arrival home. The power was out, a bare evening beckoned. The camping stove sat on the cold cooker, candle in saucer, jacket on. Later an unexpected electronic ping, and there was light. The boiler clumped into action, pipes ticking. Quiet fell more rain, pattering on glass. A rook cawed, the pen scratching on paper.

Up the valley at Rushbanks Farm, six roe deer pushed from valley-floor spinney by the rising river were grazing in the meadow. Farmer Garth Bates stopped to talk about deer and cattle, the wood never flooded before. It was disturbing. He and the other family farmers of the valley have gathered up animal feed to drive west to the Levels. Cattle cannot come back: no one dares let TB jump east. Those farmers must sell, the prices on the floor.

The rain dashed in again. The valley was a swamp, trees wandering out into new lakes.

The power failed again. No wonder the company boss moved quickly out of the village. In the garden a pencil cypress had tipped too far, and would come down. The log fire glowed, the only source of inside heat. The tree fell under the ceaseless saw. A robin hopped up, a meter away, then inches. It tipped its head, one way then the other. Feathers were ruffled in the wind.

Planing buzzards called. There was moss to scratch away from lawn, invasive wild garlic to clear from daffodil and crocus. Pulling weeds, soaking up rare sun. Autumn leaves had covered beds all winter, now were raked in piles. The soil warmed. It was a time for watching, to note each plant and bird. Flocks of tit and goldfinch were at the feeders. Robins have learned to hover inside a blur of wings, and swoop away. A woodpecker laughed. After all the work and aches, it was a time for simply sitting in the sun and reading. Now came a honeybee, and another. Two years ago, there were none all year. Many midge swarmed, a ladybird crawled across the page.

> An owl hooted, in the full flush of daylight,
> Unhinged by hints of spring.
> After the rain came mist, razored away by morning sun.
> The garden was singing.
> Above were vocal buzzards.
> Come north, swift and swallow, there is much for you already.

Last week, a sparrowhawk dashed across the garden, swerving fast, and was gone. The next day, driving down the valley: two more sparrowhawks perched on posts, and a peregrine flashed fast over field. The land had come alive.

———◦———

13. THE BEACH CROWS

The east wind tore up the Thames, the estuary gone to sickly green. White horses raced wildly at the city. Boats were tight on anchor chains, waiting out the storm. On this side was Southend's iron pier, if vertical, higher than Britain's tallest mountain. It was closed, again, a careless captain, said the press, but hard to miss. Planners built the pier for paddle steamers and those caged in city smogs: in the late 1940s, 7 million summer visitors walked the red carpet. They drank down their hard-won wages, the town prospered.

Now the promenade was abandoned, the beach empty. Music leaked from amusement arcade, where the house always wins, flickering light in displays named from afar: Electric Avenue, New York, Monte Carlo, Las Vegas. On the far side was the giant Isle of Grain chimney, tall to push away pollution, the marshes all around under acquisitional gaze of the mayor who wants a London airport here. We will fight, say locals on the Hoo Peninsula. One way or another, someone will lose their air. The economy must have it. In the estuary had been dredged a seventy-five-kilometer channel for the world's largest container ships, soon to thud upriver to the London Gateway port.

Much shipping for more shopping.

There were many development plans, one needing just the few billion for a tunnel of concrete tubes to Kent. No one mentioned the environment much. No one worried about the wrecks of the *London* and *Richard Montgomery*, stuffed with high explosive. Two years ago, bomb disposers blew up war ordnance on the beach. The coast guard said it was at *a very remote location*, seeming to imply it was not.

Out east was Thorpe Bay and distant Maplin Sands. Recent times have seen red mullet at the pier, a pilot whale in the estuary. Pollution control has made the Thames the cleanest metropolitan river in Europe. Low over dashing waves, a flock of nervous redshank flitted in and out of the world. Brent geese paddled west towards the pier, down from Greenland for the winter. Waves crashed over boat ramp, sandpiper dancing back and forth amongst bladder wrack. The British Gas building was being demolished, another block that planners once proudly deployed to fill the town's bomb plots, the breaker's ball smashing through the concrete. Many blocks in the town stand empty, windows stoned from afar. *Hotel Opportunity*, said a sign on the hoardings. Close view of airliners, maybe.

Back on the beach, crows and black-headed gulls argued over rows of seaweed, searching for sandhoppers. Some beach crows are known to have copied waders, probing for food far out on the mud. Now one crow juggled up a cockle in its beak, beating up thirty feet. It hovered, moved over stone, dropped the shellfish. It swooped to eat, too fast for gathered gulls. Many are the reports of clever corvids, but this was new. Another flew up into the wind and did the same. The shell fell and cracked. The crow ate.

There was no one else watching. No visitors, no locals. A ragged older bird was perched on the roof of a closed café. It took off, the wind ripping it into a flagpole with a clang. It clung on, bobbing with embarrassment.

Inland, spring-messenger celandine and lemony primrose had appeared in hedge banks. Hazel catkin danced on the wind. Above sang skylark, above them flew a river of rook. In the house, an angry queen wasp buzzed, flying fast and free when the window opened. Camellia buds were green and nearly pink, the limey delphinium near a foot tall.

—⟪⟫—

14. SOME SPRING FOR CELANDINE

It was some spring for celandine. We had learned patience, this long winter that stole the soul. There was a glimpse of warmth when sun broke at dawn. But in raced cold, snowflakes drifted, temperature too low for plants to grow.

Fast, though, came birds, responding to longer days. A flock of twenty siskin squabbled in the birch, green and yellow by flaky white bark. On the feeders were goldfinch and heavy greenfinch, blue and great tit, a rare coal tit. A family of long-tailed tits swooped in, balls of feathers, hanging upside down. The finch is a messy feeder, flipping out every other sunflower seed. Dunnock and blackbird waited below.

A tiny muntjac was in the garden, browsing on heather.

That deer will grow large in time.

In the kitchen was soup for lunch,

A mouth sore from dental sorcery.

The other day,

The neighborhood's fat ginger cat had a chaffinch in its jaw.

Some fields were too wet for the harrow. In others, winter cereals hesitated at the four-leaf stage. First hawthorn leaves were faint green. Along the undulating valley road, the five-mile corridor to Bures, skylark sang above the meadows. It had always been so.

In the village church, a day of celebration for the valley's finest author. Ninety then, Ronald Blythe writes and gardens every day, his next book tense at proofing stage. There were talks and readings by Richard Mabey, James Canton, famed voice actor David Holt, storytelling of the pike, the chill heart of winter, and the fish deep in the shadows of the bleak river. In an armchair on the stage, Ronnie sat in front of Constable's altar painting. The audience hunched in hats and coats. A green leafy fellow stared from the eaves, oak leaves sprouting from his mouth, this pagan missed by warring Parliamentarians who knocked the cross from off the steeple. Days later, I picked up Ronnie and we drove to the university for Richard's lecture on Essex edgelands, weeds pushing through concrete and invaders to be celebrated.

> Down deep lane to the thatched farmhouse,
> The headlamps flitted over a tawny haunting the night.

Forecasters said it will have been the coldest March, just three degrees, quite unlike last year's heat and hosepipe ban. Celandine barely had a chance. Snowdrop still were in fine fettle. On the camellia near the back door was a single flower, brightly facing south.

———◆———

15. BLACKTHORN DAYS

On just two days of the year does day length equal night. The equinox passed, the clocks changed, there was an extra bright hour of evening. It was the time of smiles. In the garden, the camellia bloomed magenta, honeysuckle and rose sprouting, all else thankful for a dry spring without slugs. Many birds came, the feeders full, nest boxes awaited.

Hedgerows up and down the valley revealed the erratic arrival of warmth and light. A few hawthorn, leafing first then flowering in May, were a blur of lime foliage; most were still dormant. In a good year, *Prunus* dominates March landscapes with icing-sugar spray. Many call them blackthorn, *Prunus spinosa*, but mostly this is mistaken. Blackthorn forms spiny thickets, one or two flowers together. The eye catches the cherry plum, *Prunus cerasifera*, and related varieties of Japanese cherry. Flower hunters scoured nineteenth-century Asia, sending back plum samples from Central Asia to the Balkans, cherry from Tibet to Japan. Many escaped gardens for hedgerows: Yoshino, Hokusai, Shimidsu, Tai-Haku, Ukon, Kanzan. In Japan, cherry blossom ceremonies are the deep meaning of spring, the flowers bringing people together and petals drifting on the breeze, profound reminders of impermanence. But that part of the deal did not come. The previous year, the world watched open-mouthed at the tsunami in Japan, recorded in real time by phone cameras, all reminded too of brutal nature as well as beauty.

Morning mist and bleached cloud cleared, and we walked from Arger Fen's woodland west. Above parched wheat was the torrent of skylark song. The path rose over glacially rounded hills, dropped to a wetland wavering with lapwing, climbed to the thatched stone chapel where Edmund was hurriedly crowned. It was an unusual path, still used as a route to get places.

> There was cherry plum intense with sprays,
> And solitary bees in blackthorn blossom,
> A promise of bitter sloes for autumn gin.
> It is a hard wood, good for walking sticks,
> In hedge banks were bluebell,

Cow parsley, and dog's mercury,
On the path people striding fast.

By a farm reservoir, soon to be in demand this spring, circled a buzzard. On the far side of the valley, sunlight glinted silver on thin glider wings, riding its own thermals.

—————

16. THE BLUE LIGHT OF SPRING

The electric hint did not persist. In came pewter-gray sky, locked low cloud, biting northeasterlies dashing far from lands of ice. A pair of ink-black rooks probed a field of curdled clay. It was too cold for scent, all sucked from out the land. Then one field on the valley floor was smeared with sewage sludge, awaiting the plow, clutching at throat, even more than the economy.

There had been powdered snow on north-faced hedge and brown furrow, over-flows from ditch stilled by ice and frozen over roads.

At wetlands on the Brett were a hundred whistling wigeon,
Their calls caught between flat sky and gray water.
They rose in a mist of swirling wings,
Fell back to choppy water.
There was a single saffron daffodil,
Awaiting warmth.

From pylons came the song of a giant. At a distance it suggested strange birds, but here was a soundscape far wider than one horizon. Once electricity passed by rural villages for decades before cottagers could afford to be connected. Now high-voltage cables had become a stringed instrument, a ping accelerating from one horizon toward the other. Miles beyond were workmen, stranded high and raw, banging out a song of despair.

We traveled to the city, the air cold and train quiet. We walked past the gold-topped Monument and crossed the river. We met Freya and Theo at the base of the tallest tower, built on oil, the glass Shard slicing the top of the sky. They had left their homes minutes before. The lifts were fast, ceiling, wall, and floor all video screens, a moment to remember an ascent of the World Trade Center, made just months before the end. This day, mist had closed off the distance, yet still the world city of nearly two thousand separate square miles was laid before us. Below were crawling trains and the tiny London Eye, nature in roof garden and secret tennis court, trees in ground-level corner park and churchyard. There were old haunts, current flats, Olympic Park itself appearing close, the hospital by the river where they each were born. On the Thames were standing waves where muddy inrush tide met outbound river, and on the far bank, blocking the skyline further, the concave walkie-talkie that come summer would focus sunlight and melt cars below. A plane for London City roared and dived for the dockland. There were cranes, more than in all the rest of Britain, said a recent report.

We leant onto the glass and looked down, heads swimming. Such is the effect of longing for spring, for the economy to recover too.

At street level, the original St. Thomas' Hospital was open. Beyond a sealed roof door, the operating theater with wooden viewing gallery had been forgotten for a hundred years. It was austere, scrubbed of bloody stain, anesthetic invented only in the 1850s. There were display cases filled with shiny devices, knife, clamp, saw. The man with anemic skin and slick black hair bid us good-bye with a twisted smile. At a restaurant by the river, thin sun shone on the frothy water.

One day, the trapdoor tipped.
It spilled the blue light of spring.
The mist of morning lifted and crystal sunlight blushed the land
With promise.

APRIL

17. TWO BUZZARDS

Far, far away, two buzzards spiraled in sapphire sky. A hooting rook climbed from the valley and mobbed them. The buzzards planed upwards, mewing, becoming small, the tiny corvid laboring to the south. The east country has red kite too, both self-spread from the west, outdating bird guides, breeding on platform nests in craggy willow, and reshaping rabbit numbers.

A planned bird introduction was canceled from Whitehall. White-tailed eagles hunt on Scotland's rocky shore, once were here too. James Wentworth Day wrote of sea eagle over Geedon Marsh in the 1930s. The minister's tidings: these birds will pounce on piglets. His other job: local pig farmer, big man. They take dead lambs in the Highlands, enough to worry but not yet a pig. Before dismay, delicious irony. Eagles might come without visas: a pair flew from Germany, staying six months in the Blyth Valley; another lingered up at Corton. Next year, they would settle at Orford and on the marshy coast near Shingle Street.

> Borders for birds do not bend to political will:
> Eagles may fly, perhaps some will stay.
> That politician has already flown his post.

There was summer smog in the city, out here days and more days of sun. Bluebell had blossomed, nightingale yet to blow in. Rape splashed fields pepper yellow; in others wheat was a foot tall. Early oak were olive green, lacy parsley stitched to roads. Yet daffodil were still in flower, celandine too. In the garden, young delphinium so far escaped slug and snail. There were early signs of drought out on the heathlands, where free-range pigs slumped, arum lily were crisp as paper. This day last year was low, strong north wind, a wall of rain. Now, dew at night saves many plants.

Mid-evening I drove to the station to wait for my daughter's train. Gray-faced commuters staggered, others smiled to friends. Earlier, hanging baskets had been planted, and foxglove transferred to the garden's shady edge. The brown bin was full with lilac wood, alive last year then suddenly dead. Honeysuckle and climbing rose by the front door were bright green. Then heavy work, carrying double glazing to the garage, a job coming around with greater regularity as the years pass.

By the back door two nights in succession, a tawny quavered. Up at the timber yard, guinea fowl creaked at roost, wary of prowling foxes.

—◦◦◦◦◦◦—

18. THE LONG NIGHT OF HOPE

After cold came the glow of frozen stone. After heavy rain, gray skies and gloom. One long pause and another sober wait. A gale, a gust, the forecast watched with hope.

Then sunshine and warmth, for nearly hours. More planting for the coming spring. Two hundred pots were now lined up, on bench and seat and table. Soil was on hands and arms, the back creaking. Shadow faded and cloud raced in. The rain speckled leaves again. For two nights pots were reclothed in plastic, by morning all crackled with frost. Doves wheezed; a green woodpecker cackled.

But it was the alchemy of change. Continental air advanced northward, a froth of yellow-green appearing on willow. Late blackthorn burst icing in the hedgerow now lime with hawthorn too. A hare stood bold in the middle of a road, skylark hovered and pigeon squabbled. A single glossy bird crowed from a furrowed field of clods.

> Late April and no sign of dazzling fields of yellow.
> Bumblebees flew out of synchrony:
> There were too few flowers.
> Cow parsley was rising,
> Anemone dashing too. It would be a second summer
> Without a honeybee.

On the train back from a long ride, there were beery sports fans in blue. The bike stand was by the toilet, a queue snaked the whole hour. There was loud singing, mostly at the enemy in yellow and green from over the county border. Parents wanted to cover children's ears, tried not to display dismay. Confident were those in blue. Later, the score; they lost 5–1 at home. The greatest rivals are usually the closest neighbors. There is little worse than dashed hope, except perhaps no hope.

It was briefly warm, twenty degrees by mid-afternoon, a taste of arid summer. At late evening, long after milling insects had departed and the last thrush had sung, there was aroma from wooden chairs and night-scented phlox. Magenta flowers were bright on the bottle-green camellia. Shoals of clouds raced from the moon, the night now silver. Eight hundred years ago, Dōgen Zenji wrote, "When body and mind are not at ease, thorns grow."

After years of sunny service, the trampoline had to be dismantled, and a new plan made for the bottom of the garden. At the estuary have been heard nightingale, and someone has caught the call of cuckoo. The thrush sang from treetop: just come.

An artist school friend, Paul, smallholder now in the Welsh hills, penned a proper longhand letter, talking of the Hay Festival and learning by heart Eliot's *Four Quartets*. "This is proving difficult," he said, "more than I had imagined." Then he finished, "Let me know when the next Ramblings of a Suffolk Boy become available." He pours a dram of delusion. "Perhaps we'll do well in the football," he concluded of England.

———◦———

19. MYSTERY SOLVED

An insect mystery solved. Black flies swarmed at apple blossom, over rape field and wet grassland were bibionids. True flies, related to midge and mosquito, hairy and black, stout antennae and spiny tibia. The heavy adults do not feed, their role in pollination curious. Last year, they were abundant in April too: so this drought has not disrupted their synchronous emergence. At this time, cycling is best undertaken with a closed mouth. A bibionid was snatched up to carry home to identify, but by a field of shimmering rape, an early wasp lodged inside my shirt. A passing car slowed, faces turned to watch.

We went north for literary lunch. Someone said there is always sunshine at Snape. But like the beach and haymaking, you tend to choose less often under gray sky. Thus do events and places become located in the bright sun of memory. Richard Mabey gave an introduction, I talked about the book of the coast, we ate. A few days later, there was a chat at Browsers bookshop and café. Liz Calder started, thirty people crammed on stools and chairs by shelves of real books. Outside rain sluiced on shiny cobbles.

One afternoon, Theo messaged to say he was in a midland town, at the football. We needed a single win to escape relegation. The radio chattered in the garden as young plants were potted on, the pale patter of raindrops on leaves a gentle song. We lost in the final few minutes.

A cuckoo called from on our hill.

Late last summer, I was stung inside the lip up on the dragon mount. The bee sting lodged. It was a day for grain dryers, roaring over the land, barley fields harvested and already plowed brown. Wheat was stiff and golden. A taste of rain was in the air. The venom shock reverberated, the swelling fierce. For days, my face was as numb as from any dental effort.

That same day, a book review was published in London, containing my line about not seeing a honeybee all summer. And there it was, the only one.

> How reluctantly
> The bee emerges from deep
> Within the peony.
>   Matsuo Bashō, 1644–1694

———⟪⟫———

20. NIGHTINGALES AND GREEN MEN

In no other land could this happen. The hours before dawn were warm and angels might be up the valley. Pale cow parsley emerged from sunken lanes, filled too with liquid song of robin. Andrew and Penny Phillips drew up, daughter Caitlin too, at the edge of Arger Fen and Tiger Hill, all whispering as before theater curtains. It was a land of ancient woodland, grand wild cherry and fissured oak, acid grassland and meadow grazed by muscled cattle. It was a dawn for budding naturalists, Tristan and Marco, aged eight and ten. It was a route from wild to the heart.

> And there,
> Right away,
> In thicket of cherry plum and blackthorn
> By a pit dug for the brick of laborer's cottage:
> Buzzing,
> Ever inventive,
>
> The song of nightingale.

There were smiles in the gloaming. They had swift flown from winter in West Africa; numbers said to be down. Yet here in north Essex and south Suffolk they were back, to Fingringhoe Wick by the Colne, onward to the valley too. The melodious song is rich, penetrating, mixed whistles, drums, and chuckles. Hesitations as well: Richard Mabey has written, "It's a performance made up, very often, more of silence than utterance."

The weft of the day was complete, though rising before four had seemed risky. There was more song: little owl whoop, tawny hoot, cuckoo far off, green woodpecker. Species of flowering plant were counted too. More interested in things to hold, the boys grabbed up insect and caterpillar, popped them in jars with magnifier tops. A roe deer barked repeatedly. Hawthorn dripped the perfume of champagne, bluebell dyeing the smoky dawn blue beneath the trees. Tristan found a black dorbeetle, taking it as a glossy pet. Marco leapt when a silver slow worm slid by his mother's foot. They wanted to hold it, hopping with excitement. Nature is not for looking at; it's for being in, playing with.

"Too many times," wrote Robert Finch at his *Outlands*, "have I seen schoolchildren marched through natural places and wildlife refuges in hushed reverence." Parents today often forbid children from engaging in wild play, quite forgetting that in disobeying their parents they learnt this way when young.

> Every child should climb trees,
> Make dens,
> Dam brooks,
> Pick up insects,
> Push out frontiers from the known worlds.

As morning brightened, a maple tree shed black rain of a thousand bibionids. The pagan boys snapped off oak fronds, held them over faces, becoming Green Men.

A long time later, we sat on logs by crackling fire, clutching coffee and buns of blackened bacon, pitying the young royal couple in London. Unlike these boys, they would never go free range again, nor will their children. The nightingales were singing as we departed. At home, clothes reeked of ash smoke. How many dawns pass without notes of such splendor?

Caitlin sent a scanned copy of "The day I saw a slow worm," Tristan's account for school.

He had written, "It was like we were in a brand new world, a world of peace and happiness & wonder. It was an amazing sensation."

21. SAILORS' READING ROOM

Cries from the beach. The crunch of waves. Three dongs from the clock on the north wall, the wooden echo of tick and tock, tick and another tock. Sunlight streamed from upper windows. The room was empty yet filled with the silence of centuries. Along the seafront were Easter visitors, zips pulled up tight. Insects were flighting on the breeze.

On the walls inside the airy Reading Room were pictures of men of the sea, chin beards and clay pipes, long gazes through camera to far horizons. The fishermen were also staring at the end of a way of life. There were beach yawls, gaff-rigged and clinker-built, oyster trawls and well smacks. There were models of naval vessels with tall sails and later gunmetal: lost in the Battle of Solebay, then to oily U-boats scalping the shore of fishermen and their ways of life.

The clock tocked on.

Once were longshoremen in sou'westers mending nets, boys watching, women walking while they knitted, boats rowed from the harbor, others crashed on the sand. In paintings were standing groups watching as they would never do in a real storm. The name *Nordharvest* was carved in gold letters on a fragment of wood hung above the door, a boat from Thule, somewhere cold and dark in winter, just as icy on the seabed.

The Reading Room was opened 150 years ago and has looked on change. Thirty years back, in this very space, I experimented with angled Rodchenko-style monochromes, the sunlight sharp and shadows deep. Today the floor was still red linoleum, the sky outside blue. Along the front, scaffolding was hung on our old house, builders and painters clumping out of an unguarded front door. Fifty years ago, we were running into freedom, down to the beach, salt frying on our skin. Now years have passed. There was no way back through the door, open though it appeared.

Four figureheads looked on, their heads tipped to one side, eyeline above the sealine, as if sky mattered more than water. It was warm and still subdued, the sea brushing at the shore. A dog yelped; a man walked in, grimaced, searching his wallet for a code, slipping through a secret paneled door. The room was empty, save for the sweet air of sea and memories, in the distance cries of happy children.

---

22. THE ASSINGTON ELMS

This thirsty spring, one leaf was still asleep. Skeletal ash say dry summer. The oaks were green. A country saying scans: "Oak before ash, we're in for a splash; ash before oak, we're in for a soak." Splash it was then.

But elms beg attention. Under fungal pressure, they evolved from trees to spindly hedgerow shrubs. Constable painted the valley's elms, towering trees that defined an English rural idiom. The laureate of the Essex marshes, Samuel Bensusan, wrote that the *ellum* was prone to throw out a heavy branch in a storm. Now many east country hedges are dense with stretches of toothed foliage with the irregular leaf base. Most elm species produce only suckers, forming identical clones. No wonder they fell to relentless Dutch elm disease.

By the close of the 1970s, the timeless tree was gone. There was no dose, the crime was done. William Dutt walked in Suffolk a century ago: "In almost every part of the county oak, ash, black poplar and elm grow freely by the roadside and along field boundaries." The first survives, the next soon threatened, the third rare, and the elm is felled. Ronnie Blythe has written, "Bereaved elm-lovers continue to walk the land in tears."

White-spotted pinions were lost too, big-eyed micro-moths that feed only on elm. The east's last official record was in 1980; then in summer of 2013, three were found at the reserve on the Colne, close to that glossy ibis.

There were some resistant survivors. Two elms on Assington High Street, one up Gravel Hill in Nayland, a row of a dozen east of Hadleigh at Elmsett, one survivor on the windy path to St. Peter's Chapel on flat Dengie. The scientific hero of elm, R. H. Richens of Cambridge, wrote that elms have been "taxonomically recalcitrant for three hundred years." Put another way, they are very variable. The English elm never crossed a line east of Bedford to Kent, so our elm is wych elm, the only species able to produce seedlings. At the new house in Assington with the mature adult in the front garden, the man shrugged. "No idea. Try the old farmer down the road?" But never once a response to knocks at the old door, and perhaps no answer was the answer.

Assington was named in the Domesday Book, once had four manors and a grand hall, was dominated by wool merchants, and took a radical turn in 1845, when John Gurdon fused the village into a Digger agricultural cooperative. The Assington Society issued local currency, built brick houses, encouraged local food and internal trade. It flourished to 1918, then the social economy was undermined, or just ran out of time; the hall fell to fire in the late 1950s, like many others. The elms survived. A billion deciduous trees in Britain, and now more threat: leaf miner on horse chestnut, *Phytophthora* on alder.

But there was another chapter, another shock. No one in the UK had yet heard of ash dieback.

MAY

23. THE OWL AND THE SUN

Let us speak of a gray day.
Even as the sun tore a hole in the flat morning,
A little owl was on the road,
Pecking at an ounce of rabbit.

A waxed utility vehicle raced on regardless, clipping the carcass. The pocket owl staggered, swerved into the hedge, and flashed across the field. It shrank above the dusty soil, was gone.

The next morning,
Tall cow parsley shivering at the same verge,
A pheasant rose and clutched at air,
And flew at another car with a thump.
It was gone.

These were the weather signs that particular spring. Satellite maps said it might rain. Unlikely: all had forgotten what wet was. On the solar panels was a carpet of red silt fallen from the Sahara. The data were still fine, the house registered as a power station. How good if every roof had solar, selling to the grid, emitting nothing to the air. We joined a social enterprise in the village, now installing eighty-four panels on the school roof. The next generation may know what to do.

It had been the hottest April on record. Lawns were scenes of scorched summer. The garden wanted water, a time for watching allium appear, the delphinium stronger than any year, Japanese anemone also racing up. But a pittosporum shrub blinked after the bone cold: every leaf fell in two days. Then the camellia crisped off. Buckets of water were rushed out before a dash to speak at a spring festival. It was a mardle in a dusty barn, a coastal celebration of place and food, the audience sitting on sofas and farm chairs.

On return, the red moon was hanging huge over dry dark trees. Driving slowly with the windows wide, the warm country night cried and called.

On the long road north, Bashō wrote:

> Heard, not seen
> The camellia poured rainwater
> When it leaned.

—————

24. THE BAT AND THE WILD

The bat did come back. Each evening that week, a pipistrelle put a spell on the garden. It banked in silence, trawling insects, slipped away. Once a bright moth labored over pepper broom: pop, it was a shower of dust and cell. The bat flew on. At the time, robin was at evensong, blackbird chip-chipping alarm calls at prowling cats. From a nearby garden came shouts of laughing children, outdoors instead of in. Tonight, heavy clouds hurried from the west, yet the gibbous moon was bright. Each night, it migrates back by eighty minutes. Full moon in four days.

> One night like this,
> The moon waxing so,
> A bat bit through my bloody thumb.

But the bat was welcome wild. In a domestic garden, scarlet rose and tall foxglove shiver together, the land so managed yet the weeds and wild still come. Sixty species of bird in or over the garden. The leading twitchers tick off four hundred, but still, not so bad. This lovely land, both wild and managed, side by side and interweaved. Along the valley floor are creamy Charolais and brown South Devons. There are ridged plots of Maris Peer and Charlotte potato, far fields of onion. Farms in Suffolk and Essex shooting game have on average 7 percent of land under woodland; farms that do not have just 1 percent. Many are the pheasants and partridge. Our choices on garden and farm management matter.

Two plans were the talk of the valley: one to drop a theme park with wrecking retail on the Essex tops; the other, to extend this Area of Outstanding Natural Beauty west and north up-valley. Constable would have approved the latter, local villagers were up in arms about the former. Bright posters appeared in front windows and on lampposts. There were meetings in front rooms, strategies for planners at the borough council. The developers set up Suffolk Punch horses by their pub, but trying to be traditional did not hide destructive intention. They believe they are being good.

But the land was in more immediate jeopardy. The bat took the moth, the saw-ing buzz of stag beetle awaited. The fields were parched, clay soils fissured. March was the driest and hottest on record, less than a twentieth average rainfall. Barley and rape were in torment, thin and discolored. It was the same in northern France. The Mediterranean climate was marching north, it seemed. Outside two bats flew across the moon. The garden welcomed the grace of nightly dew. Where would the world be, always bereft:

> O let them be left, wildness and wet;
> Long live the weeds and the wilderness yet.
> Gerard Manley Hopkins,
> 1844–1889, "Inversnaid"

---

25. TIME TRAVEL

Officials declared drought. Hosepipes were banned, water anxiety grew. Reporters stood in empty reservoirs. There will be the effort of carrying cans and pails, perhaps all summer for allotmenteer and gardener. Or worse, standpipe and impatient queue, as faded clips from the ill-dressed seventies remind. This spring had been strung. In the garden, still were bobbing daffodil and narcissus, three months from first bloom. The camellia had gone over, the pea shingle a carpet of fallen flowers.

Without warning came a shift. Dry heat dissolved to the gift of fronts and bub-bling storms. Thunder grumbled across the dust. A month's rain fell in a few hours, the rivers gushing fast with raging water.

Talk of drought was curbed. At dawn it was blustery, and beyond the steam-ing kettle came churr and buzz. A nightingale sang from a bush by the kitchen door. Most years, one stops awhile, pressing up-valley to summer territory. Morn-ing was for sowing seed, transplanting pots, filling hanging baskets. All received another drench, and already sun and drying wind would be welcome. The wisteria shivered. Will a plot sown with wildflower mix face much rain or searing sun? A fragrant honeysuckle and red rose have wrapped around the front door. Birds swooped to feeders, great tits taking up in the bird box at the back.

The early train to London passed fields of gray-green wheat and silvered barley, no longer drought-threatened. The heat-island effect of the city was sharply appar-ent. From outside to in was to travel forward in time. City trees and shrubs had jumped two weeks. In the park, rain lashed and umbrellas flipped, tourists gazing at damp guidebooks. Plane trees had leafed, city squares filled with lilac perfume flowered white. A ceanothus was a spray of ocean blue and cherry bloomed pink. A wet workman kicked bags of rubbish in a pile, threw them in a truck.

A quiet street was crammed with men. They held shoulder bag and stepladder, wearing black windcheater, cameras under cover. They waited for the media tycoon, called to account before the House of Commons inquiry. In Japan, the camellia is a flower with cultural significance, falling not by petal but as a whole flower. Rather like, they say, the severing of a person's head, or the sudden loss of a leader of an organization. But this man put shameless blame on junior staff, coming out all the stronger.

Back home, the fête was on the village green. Straw bales, canvas snapping, racing cloud, people hanging onto hats, the beer tent busy, jazz quartet tapping feet. Children were called forward by age group, girls then boys, for flat-out running, then egg and spoon and three-legged race. The sack race was back in hessian, last year's bin liners fast forgotten. There was plant and book stall, wooden balls to throw at coconut and crockery, tea and cake in hall, and wild food too.

A mile down-valley at Tendring Hall had lived the Norfolks. One typical day, the duke and duchess and three visitors slaved hard to keep the wolf from the door. It was capon and beef for breakfast; for a ten o'clock dinner, two capon boiled, mutton, beef, a swan, a pig, veal, and two more capon roasted and a custard; second course, salmon from the river, pigeon, rabbit, shoveler, oystercatcher, a dozen quail, and pasty of venison and pear; supper at five o'clock: mutton, rib of beef, another swan and capon. The hall later fell into disrepair, then was used to house German and Italian prisoners of war in the 1940s. The Italians were expert poachers, snaring game and songbird. But the hall could not survive: it too burned in the 1950s.

A local chef had traveled back in food time, with fête marquee for wild food collected from within a mile or ten: crayfish and perch, rabbit and glasswort, pigeon and venison, pheasant and dandelion. Children gathered round, adults too. What crazy wildness: it might make us look anew at food and land.

Wrote Lao-tzu:

> Fields are overgrown
> Granaries are empty
> But the nobles' clothes are gorgeous.

—◁◁◁▥▯◁▯▥▷▷▷—

26. SINCE RECORDS BEGAN

It was the wettest month since records began. Well, for a hundred years. For the southeast, 65 percent more rain than average. Variability is not new: old farmers remark on weather events never seen before in their lifetime. Yet average seems antiquated when weather patterns have been spiced with industrial unpredictability.

Last weekend, angry clouds tore in from the south. Atlantic fronts crashed into Spain and France, then were diverted here by high pressure. In the north, it has been cold and often sunny.

Under Queen Anne, an act of Parliament was passed in 1705 to make "the river Stower navigable." One hundred commissioners, each peer and baronet, knight and squire, were appointed to referee disputes between riparian owners and improvers. Just nine were needed for a cozy quorum. As with transport infrastructure today, local interests rarely prevailed against the march of trade and growth. There were punishments for people injuring navigation: for opening a staunch, or throwing stone and timber in the river, three months' hard labor. For 150 years, industrialists ran river barges up- and down-valley, then came a rail century until Beeching's hurried cuts, and now the age of motorcar.

This age was also of Aquarius: riverbanks had burst along the valley. Water poured across meadow, through pepper rape, over wheat and barley field, across road and rill and soily potato ridge. Beneath the gray sheet of racing water was the river course. Last month a trickle ran beneath the bridge, now was a hundred meters wide, swirling and shivering, buffeting logs, pouring through fences and filling the meadow with stained sky. It was rare to see such flood. Ducks splashed where livestock had grazed. Beyond the refurbished pub, the moat around the Roman knoll was full of water. At the old lock, the river had filled the storage ponds, water lapping in the fields. There were clouds of midge. All this water so implored, soon to race fast away and irrigate the sea. There was a choice: Press on or turn back?

Wet feet were good feet. For above the swamp flashed the first swallow of spring, a dozen dashing low, chittering through the midges. Adults glided with long tail streamers, first-year juveniles beating hard. They had come so far, a dangerous narrative of migration, now returned to hunt, the same village eaves to nest. This for them was half a home.

In the garden, apple had flowered, a glimpse of evening sunlight brushed rose on petals under purple sky. Six more patches were planted with wildflower; sun might bring butterfly and honeybee. Overhead came the rumble of war engine, and a Lancaster droned across the sky, heading for an air show at the sandy coast. Foxglove bobbed bright, attracting bumblebee but blackfly too.

At dusk, we searched for other migrants up the hill where roamed that sabered tiger. The evening was damp and timeless. We walked into woodland of wet oak and scrubby elm. The bank of bluebell, last year scorched and gone over, was a haze of lilac fog and stitchwort petals pure white on stems of filigree. There was a thrush singing in the oak top, blackbird and robin, chiff-chaff, many pheasant and chaffinch, a distant peacock, many mosquito. But no nightingale. They were silent. It was too wet.

Yet there were roe deer, ears splayed, eyes probing in the dusk. Down in a swidden between woods on each side of the valley, a male barked roughly, an archaic spirit in an ancient wood. Soon the hinds will give birth to speckled twins, always one fawn male and one female. Britain has more deer than since the Domesday Book: no natural predators, more woodland, not much human poaching. Roes are originals, here since the Mesolithic. They have been around since, well, records began.

Night fell. A fox's eyes glittered in the headlight. This dim world was about to become darker.

---

27. BELLS IN THE COW PARSLEY SEASON

Eight bells pealed, ringing changes and rolling a sonic glory across the bright churchyard and down the seaside town. The priest muttered. And so Rene Horwood's ashes were laid in the ground next to husband Don, family and friends standing under yew and holly, drowned in memory. Here are some: running in and out of their house, salt-encrusted from the beach; watching the cup final on oh-so-vivid color television in sixty-eight; talking to Rene at length about the terror of the night the North Sea tore down the town's defenses.

> In her wheelchair,
> Near-blind Avril Brown declared in Barnsley best,
> "I'll be next, but I must be sprinkled on Blackshore's rising tide.
> I want to travel the river forever."
> We breathed deeply,
> For we have done this in the past,
> And might do so again.

The flinty churchyard wall: here a seven-year-old slipped and fell into stinging nettles, wearing only shorts, it a summer day under clear sky of childhood that contained only endless sunshine, running home down the center of the street. There was soothing bath, the light and pain dulled under frosted window. Today the rich smell of brewery malt drifted from narrow streets beyond the church. Other scents unlock those times: fresh bread and fishmongers. Some memories are seared to places forever.

The roads and lanes to the north were ornamented with cow parsley. The flowers were lacy dreams in the acid green of spring, quivering on the breeze, flowing rivers in the bright air. Richard Mabey has called it Britain's most important landscape flower. The froth of bloom sings of spring, of vibrant life returned after weeping winter, of reoccurring patterns too.

These ribbons of Queen Anne's lace pose a conundrum: Have we come to value species more when they are rare? We never worried about plain old house sparrow when abundant, but their value rose as numbers fell. A single orchid is marked more than successful species. Yet without the dominance of cow parsley, spring would be poorer. At this time hawthorn were dripping with creamy bloom, fresh-scented May blossom, blended with the pepper drift of oilseed rape, yellow dazzle under blue sky.

My father was not well enough to leave home, and we drove up to St. Edmund's knapped-flint church with copper-clad roof, parking by the cottage hospital. Sunlight streamed through grand windows at the rood screen, the finest in this east country. At the west end was Southwold Jack, adopted symbol of the brewers. On each bench were carved figures, monkey preaching, beaver, man playing pipes, others from the medieval bestiary. There was reading and hymn, celebration and prayer. It had been a full life of ninety-two years.

Later, we left the hall where tea and cakes were laid on trestles, the church tall on the town center hill. We walked slowly on.

Rene always said she loved the bells.

—⁂—

28. ENCOUNTERS

I could not believe I fell asleep in a dream.
I was walking with my father,
Yet felt so tired.
Nothing in the dream was reference to any place in the known world.
I fell asleep,
But was already asleep.

Outside it was almost possible to breathe, the golden broom filling the garden dawn with burned scent. There was cool wind from the north, racing cloud, welcome angled sunshine. Two white butterflies trembled, settled, blue-veined on close examination. There were other whites too: rose-white of apple blossom, creamy green-white hemlock, saturated white of stitchwort. Hidden white of lilac not yet broken free. Later, standing still: a hen pheasant boldly walked to search beneath the feeders where wasteful goldfinch had fed. The bird came clucking within an inch of a palm spread with sunflower seed, bobbing, settling, almost taking then turning away. Three times it edged closer. All breath was frozen, the hand steady.

The ginger cat exploded from the shrubs. The bird clattered up, a phoenix clutching at the air, the dream over. The cat calmly trotted around the house.

Black bibionid flies had come, much later than usual, and bumblebees caromed over bushes. Overhead hurried a hawk. A skylark hovered inside its spring song. On one drive to work, two jackdaws were investigating chimney pots. They too hovered, over each pot, looking down, checking for signs of heat before risking feet. That evening, walking the garden to check on recent plantings: there beneath the dripping hawthorn was a pile of pigeon down. Here had come the violence of a stooping falcon. Pigeon had been at the hostas, pecking such damage it had suggested an army of snail.

It was blustery, and a new nature reserve was to be opened. I drove my mother down to the Thames shore. On a twenty-meter hill by the gray river stood a giant marquee large enough for two thousand visitors. They had come to hear a man who had for sixty years brought wildlife from every continent to television screen. Below was the moody river, model for Conrad's distant *Heart of Darkness*, nearby his house at Stanford-le-Hope. Here we were, at Mucking, on top of Essex's largest garbage tip. Once were clouds of gulls, plastic snagged in every hedgerow, the trucks miniature on the waste mountain ditched by people of London. The Essex marshes had always been remote enough from the city to be a place for waste. Now those days were over. But stuff will still be thrown away. To the east towered the first batch of blue cranes at the Gateway port, where more will arrive by container ship.

Here, though, was green meadow spread out as a fine prairie. A textured landscape under an immense sky, "an ocean of wind-troubled grass," Wallace Stegner wrote. Skylark, adder, carder bee, wasp spider, avocet, redshank and barn owl, newt and orchid, cuckoo and wagtail, all were here, rarities and commonalities, gathered already on a land transformed by Essex Wildlife Trust. I introduced Sir David Attenborough to the audience, and bent by years and disheveled by wind he voiced concerns and spoke of this fragile world. He waved his arms to celebrate what here had been achieved, where time's arrow had reversed direction. Visitors grinned, held up mobile phones. There was much warmth, even as a squall battered at the snapping canvas. On return, trees and shrubs were racing nowhere, swaying, trembling, awaiting the warmth of summer. June approached, the month of midsummer, and some trees had barely leafed.

One of Bashō's last haiku, written a month before his death aged only fifty, seemed appropriate. Out of darkness comes sound; out of dark also comes light. Such is the nature of deepest experience.

> A flash of lightning;
> Into the gloom
> Goes the heron's cry.
> Matsuo Bashō,
> 1644–1694

---

29. THE NORTHERN SKY

A miracle in the modern sky: twenty-foot cypress next door have been downed, taken from the north, and now light let in. Birds swoop longer distances, plants that never felt the drench of rain are wet. The wind blows harder. The tree man was careless, the mallow crushed. But the light at evening was brighter, the day longer. That pink mallow should come again.

At evening, a single bat darted through the gloaming. Then a dawn shock. A huge rook perched on the feeders. The first time ever settling in the garden. More came. The next night brought a parched nightmare, walking as if in a pitiless desert.

Another evening after the trees went down, a nightingale sang graceful from the hill. It chirped to midnight. In the morning it had advanced to the garden, in the camellia. Singing to a sky that was so marvelous.

As I wrote, a solitary bee flew up and rested on my arm. Then it sat on the warm wood bench, quivering in the sunshine. An orange-tipped butterfly flew to purple lilac. Just one rose was in blossom, the lemon aromatic brought from Brixton Hill thirty years ago.

Again a nightingale sang, now under creased skies where dark clouds had been and rain still fell. There was space on the land for bleating sheep, cranky geese, creaking guinea fowl. Robin and blackbird fell silent. Dark advanced. Still the bird sang. The tawny owl hooted. A second nightingale joined to the east. The sky was vast without those trees. The moon rose, and all the birds fell quiet.

Under night sky, beneath the round moon, a single lamb bleated.

—◦⟨∫⟩◦—

30. ALL FOUR MIGRANTS

Discovery is part of landscape. An experience of the expressed and revealed. A magic that connects with emotions. How to romance people onto the land, children especially? Fill the experience with surprise, perhaps.

The day began gray, with the promise of a dab of sun. Yet later the cloud peeled away as the bells of VE Day rang, the song too of post-election sorrow and the blue streaked with high trails of hope. A day of skylark rapids, flood of song from safety between gray-green wheat and the vast sky where peregrine beat.

A new route selected, over the watershed to the Colne Valley. The path was out from West Bergholt. The church was in the fields by modern barns, its bell tower tall, door locked. There were early dog walkers, a black Labrador thundering on the whistle of its walking owner. A choice: footpath through more fields or down to wood. Inside the spring forest was a blue haze. White banks of stitchwort pure on needle stems, pink of red campion, a coppiced carpet of bluebell. A sea glaze beneath oak and hazel. At the western edge was a bank of scrubby blackthorn. Woodland song, woodpecker green laughs, a greater spotted thrumming. Deer lays, plants flattened into mattresses.

And then,
The churr,
The gurgle and breathless whisper,
A resonant song more pure than any other.
A robin is silver liquid, the nightingale pure crystal.
Gemstones in the scrub,
At this time of the day,
Not dusk or dawn.

By a burbling stream was a wild patch of white garlic. The wood on the hill, Hill-house Wood, just a green shape on the map. Now populated. The migrant discover-ies had just begun. Out in the fields, the first cuckoo of spring called from the valley floor, then flighted up close. Swallow raced from one horizon. The first of spring too.

Ah, this was one day to remember.

Inside Fordham church, song was being sung, outside the graveyard bench faced north. Two swifts sliced the air, great cleavers, a tip and tuck, gone and returned. Swallows watched from wires. The butchers slid, half-a-meter wingspan, great birds but often high above and tiny to our eyes.

Down at the river, the Colne was clear, riffles bubbled as it oxbowed over vale. The sheep meadows were glossy in the sunlight, unhurried ewe and lamb mur-muring. There was warmth in the grass, a taste of summers past. Of times when time did not matter, of rivers walked with no aim, just at the end of a summer's day. Yet this older day, there were thousands of bibionid congregating by hedge and vegetation. They paid us no attention, nor the Devon cattle chewing. There were clouds of midge over the stream that ran from the patch of garlic. The bibionids will be gone by tomorrow, the midges gathered for more assault.

A farmyard was crumbling shed and asbestos roof, windows broken, machinery once shiny and promising improvement now rusted and abandoned in the nettles. The least harm will come from leaving it all be.

Back at the church, the lanes had become a car park. Families were counting children and dogs. The church was cool and quiet. There were wall paintings, clear windows, one of bleached stained glass. The tower timbers were poached with insect chambers. The wood of the last pew, compressed under gallery stairs, was carved with graffiti, initials not names. On this back row sat plowman and plasterer, reaper and milkmaid, sharing a sharp knife and sighing quietly at the sermon. It would have been about the natural order of things, them always at the back.

At home, purple aquilegia were out by pale daffodil. A sea of pink beneath camellia. There was yellow kerria, white lilac, scarlet azalea. Two blue tits dipped and swerved for the box in the honeysuckle. For the first time, flower buds on the wisteria. Each day now would bring discovery, rose and foxglove, lily and thrift, in the sky above the happy migrants.

JUNE

31. MAGIC IN THE THICKS

This is the way: when weather is warm and soils sandy, then farming without water is hard. All around, irrigation guns jetted water into the sun low over fields of purple potato. There were many rainbows. These sandlings were shrugged off in the agricultural revolution as fit for nothing but sheepwalk and layabout rabbit, yet farming today looked fine. Nearby was the Thicks, an ancient woodland of mature oak and holly, and beyond to the north, one of the county's famed singing pubs, the Green Man. Through fronds of bracken, deer and people had beaten frontier paths. Inside, the morning air was silent, the shadowed glade lanced by sun rays. Each old oak had bold bosses on fissured bark. Long ago, all were pollarded by feuding brothers arguing over the estate: so they say, each chopped out the other's leading branches. The oaks grand even then had since put out pollards ten to fifteen feet from the ground. Centuries passed, the grass grown taller, many now rotted, the heartwood dust. The girth of one was eighteen feet and must be four hundred years old, maybe older given the trauma. Some say the oyster monks of Butley Abbey were the plantsmen of the 1500s. It is good not to be sure, as for any place of myth and mystery.

The oak drew the eye, but the smooth holly were exceptional. One was the tallest in the country at seventy feet. Girths of the largest exceeded six feet. There were Siamese trees, oak-holly trunks fused by years of co-growth. On bark were names, old graffiti carved by generations long gone who walked the deep wood for an escape from high-occupancy cottages, bedrooms lacking privacy. A heart with initials; another on a rowan. A woodland for wonder, perchance to "dream, and so dream all night without a stir," wrote John Keats of oak.

These heaths were warren country, where Normans imported conies from Spain and built long mounds with artificial burrows. At the height of production, rabbit trains rattled to London carrying a million animals yearly for meat and fur. All change: they ended being useful livestock and evolved to pests. Nearby were farmed oysters, raised on creek shore since the Anglo-Saxons, sent to distant markets too.

There is more than meets the eye in these old woods: Druid ceremonies, the magic of mistletoe, strange goings-on, as they say here in the east. Great Rendlesham Forest nearby, swathes matchstick-flattened by the 1987 hurricane, was site for alien landings one Boxing Day. Flashing lights in the forest, American airmen and Suffolk police writing revealing memoranda. Down the road at Orford was a captured merman; at Shingle Street its wartime incident. There were cunning men and women, both healers and magicians. Cunning Murrell was the last wizard of Essex, born in 1780, walking the region collecting plants for cures. He slept by day, walked at night, a basket of herbs hanging from a gingham umbrella. "Do you want high or low?" he asked: magic or material help. Depicted with golden staff and feet in grass and flowers in a stained glass window, Hildegard wrote of nature and choices over high and low treatment. Thus was uncertainty explained away, and healing helped.

At garden dusk, two stag beetles whirred, clattering into birch and pencil elm as a bat slid silently in the warm air. They seemed early. The village is a hotspot, and they fly each summer, even though nationally rare. In deadwood, larvae grow for three years. More evidence that local choice in gardens and the wilds works.

The idea of a contemplative economy is appealing. If we spent more time immersed in nature, attentive too to one another, then perhaps there would be less need for material consumption. The planet could be saved, yet the economy wrecked. High magic looks to be a good choice.

—◀▥▥◯▥▥▶—

32. THE LOST SHORE

Moths fly to a night light. In the summer sunshine, people are drawn to seaside sunlight.

> Along the coastal edge,
> You come to know places by the back door,
> To find secret dune and marsh,
> Shingle and cliff,
> Serene settled,
>
> Just beyond the reach of most visitors.

Yet the seaside is new to culture. No one would have thought before two hundred years ago to sit on beach or swim in sea for pleasure. Houses up and down the coast faced inwards, fishermen and sailors not caring to look upon their cruel sea. Now it promises escape. Few of us would sit at home allowing ourselves to do nothing; yet we contentedly do so at the beach, watching others doing nothing too.

On a summer's day, when a hard nor'easterly churned the North Sea, we came to genteel Aldeburgh to record a BBC radio show on the sounds of the coast. We had been at Orford, now came to the singing shingle. In George Crabbe's day, Aldeburgh was bleak, cold, poor; Wilkie Collins thought it defenseless and desolate. Crabbe's poem, *The Borough*, was foundation for Britten's *Peter Grimes*. Beyond south Aldeburgh was the site of lost Slaughden, once port for fishermen featured by Crabbe and Britten, who sailed heroic journeys to Iceland and the Faroes and brought back cod in watery wells amidships. In their final days, fishwives opened front and back cottage doors to let the tide run in, and out. The last house was swamped by shingle in 1926; the Three Mariners Inn went under at the end of the decade. Now there is nothing. The port has wandered out to sea.

"There is no sea like the Aldeburgh sea," wrote Edward FitzGerald. "It talks to me." This day the crashing waves sucked the shingle back to sea with a cocktail crunch, then thumped back onto the shore. To swim would be to sink. On this beach was recently washed up the body parts of a large man, the mystery never solved. We crouched to record voice-over against the wave and stone.

This shore is shaped by sound. There has been a row over church bells. Incomers complained; environmental health officers stepped in: "No reason on nuisance grounds to take any action." A resident moaned, "We want silence in our garden." He had bought a house next to the church. As bell pullers ring the changes, so towers sway, flint or brick, round or square, moving to higher message, just as did step dancers ringing the rhythms on wood pub floors as accordion and fiddle played.

At the north shore beyond the fishing boats drawn up on high shingle since the port was lost, whose sun burnt tar blisters on the planks, was *The Scallop*, Maggi Hambling's sculpture corroding in the salty air. It attracted controversy, was daubed with graffiti, became quietly iconic. Children play on it. Families sit and gaze to sea. On the shelves of town shops are scallop souvenirs. Today, the waves had thrown up a haze of mist, the town to the south half-lost, battlements in the sky. To the north loomed the white dome of the nuclear power plant. A couple of years ago, the inshore lifeboat searched for a seven-year-old girl; she was found looking at *The Scallop*.

The *Four Quartets* center on the circularity of time. On this coast, erosion is forever. In some places, little is left, except memories.

> The houses are all gone under the sea
> The dancers are all gone under the hill.
> T. S. Eliot, 1888–1965

33. HOLLYHOCK SUMMER

There had been winners and losers this extreme spring and summer. Highway vandals had mowed roadside stands of cow parsley, fearful of the wild. Soon all will be down. Drought gave way to showers and hot thunderstorms, and now the summer solstice accelerated hard, the days about to shorten. One winner seems to be a pest of sixteenth-century Balkan introduction, the horse chestnut. Recent years have seen leaves rusted by Cameraria leaf miner, their first appearance as a Wimbledon wild card in 2002. The miners spread in eddies of vehicles, and by past Julys trees on roads have been scorched, leaves crisped, fast fallen to gutter. But this summer, they mostly still were green. In the garden, half a hundred cockchafer swarmed in and out of cherry trees. From over the roof others buzzed to join them. One lumbered into the kitchen, fell, stranded on the smooth floor.

A winner was the hollyhock, smuggled back by Crusaders from the East. They seed the spaces between the wild and cultivated, rising tall by stone and wall, driveway and back door, drought-resistant and flourishing in sun. They are not of flowerbeds, nor of nature reserves. They approve the edgelands, those parts untended and not designed. In Japan, the *aoi* of the mallow family were used in symbolism by the Tokugawa shogunate. There is a beauty out front, richly chocolate-flowered; out back, under the box where blue tits recently fledged, salmon hollyhocks have grown to giants, rust tearing at lower leaves.

Watering the garden is a meditation.
Look plant by plant, chart growth, watch weeds, court insects.
Listen to the birds, stare at the sky.
Settle a little more into the land.
Gardening is not about producing a crop;
It is tending each plant.
Individualizing the whole of nature is a greater task,
Yet could be vital.

The lavender swarmed with bees, on the pale thyme too. There were yellow- and red-tailed bumblebees, finely named humblebees by Richard Jefferies, and a couple of honeybees. This morning, a cuckoo called, distant and clear. Overhead a single swan thudded past, wings whistling.

A gray squirrel danced in the dry air. Fear was taught in a leap and it flashed away. On the warm step was a grass snake, silvery with yellow nape, a meter of muscle. It slid slowly after the squirrel. A moment of pride: big snake in our garden. From a neighbor's house, a string quartet played. In the 1930s, D. W. Gillingham recorded both red and gray squirrels in south Essex; in the 1950s Ambrose Waller wrote still of only reds in the Stour Valley. Yet the valiant gray ventured north and east, and soon the red was extinct.

At the valley top was a field of poppy, a layer of bloody mist above rippling silver barley. A generation ago, all cereals were long-stalked, the poppy taller too. Then came modern short varieties, the poppy flower stopping just above grain height. One evening came the grating bark of deer from the hillside. It called twenty times, stopped, and called again. Moonlight began to fill the sky. Then my mother called. An ambulance had come.

> You ask why I live
> Alone in the mountain forest,
> And I smile and am silent
> Until even my soul grows quiet.
>
> The peach trees blossom
> The water continues to flow.
>   Li Po, 701–761

⸺◦⫘⫘⫘◦⸺

34. A SUBMISSION

In a world readily atomized, it is easy to lose the connections that offer solace. Sometimes a story is not possible, at best are fractured events and observations.

By now, the road to the hospital was well ridden. Zing of car park ticket machine, animated rabble at the entrance café. But soon whisperings in airless corridors, the wards themselves gray and no saturated color and not a plant in sight. Parchment skin, agitated nurse, repeated bleep from hidden machine. A calm doctor always had a smile, set out the plan. The MRI results were painful, discussed in detail, email answered.

The nurses bustled and some seemed to be trying hard not to make eye contact.

"No change," said one with pursed lips, not looking up from the pile of paper forms and patient records.

A man on his back, everyone so thin, called me over.

"I've got to escape," he whispered, holding a hand over his mouth, urgent eyes flicking left and right. "Can you help me get to Oulton Broad?" We all need to get away from this, even if only just outside the perimeter.

A health assistant walked briskly by, from a distance shouting at another bed, "Are you in pain?"

We grimaced. Just talk, whisper amongst ourselves.

Still we roved the route. Every day to see my father. On automatic. Roads and roundabouts, hedges that had swayed with cow parsley, crops golden despite the rain. A patch of yellow tree lupin, wispy hemlock coming along too.

As worlds unravel, what was there? A submission of this saga.

For the first time in twenty years, rooks had come to the garden, cawing and crying, perched on feeders, each day from about four thirty. This morning four were on the flat roof cawing at the bedroom window. Directly, as if we were missing a message.

An experiment: canes tied to the bird feeders, pointing in the air to encourage them elsewhere. A bit of quiet in the slow dawn hours could be good. In *Crow Country* Mark Cocker wrote that rooking, the art of following and watching the birds, was not "merely about a single raucous black bird. It is about the whole world."

The hollyhock needed stakes. There were gales and the ripping of land to come. Bad at this time of year. Fully leafed trees work like sails, but cannot be reefed. Much damage was expected.

One warm morning, a greater spotted woodpecker, head blood-red, a long thin crimson tongue, was lying at the back door. A window strike, dashing at the house. The reflection of the world in the early hours was too real. It had happened to a pigeon too.

The great tits have fledged. For weeks, the adults swooped with undulating flight, paused at the nest hole, looking around, darting inside. Now, no cheeping. The red honeysuckle looked fine, some bees were swarming.

In my mother's garden, there were shades of aquilegia, purple to indigo, pink to powder blue, and snow white, now planted in my garden too. The new wildflower meadow was taking shape. The plot where once burned the rusted incinerator was invaded by two-meter nettles. Winners wherever are nutrients. Above was briefly a painter's sky. In my father's studio, all was silent. He would never paint again.

Little things help: thyme crushed between fingers, the perfume of the garrigue. Lavender brushed at night, richly filling the warm air. A white phlox, also scented.

Voices came from an open window, a television deep inside. A moth ambled by. A robin was singing, the last to sleep, first up in morning too.

The roses were coming on: red, blue-purple, apricot. The fragrant yellow, a cutting taken in those days by my mother, and passed back. But all was wet, so wet, there were few insects. Where went the summer?

Out came the sun, and in the valley heat were three groups of kids on a Duke of Edinburgh program, one striding, calling hello; the other two hunkered in the shade, many miles to finish. So drenched in sweat and tired, I was locked out. The things that can go wrong: up with the ladder and clambering through the bedroom window. In the lock on the front door were the keys.

There was financial mess on the news, one side blaming the other, the others doing the same. The butterflies in the garden were suddenly numerous. Then there was good news: we had been spending in the warm weather, using up the planet but saving the economy.

As usual, the wheels had fallen off the national football team in the finals.

Someone wrote: note ten things a day that take your full attention, that make you, well, happy. This is a good exercise, though ten is often hard.

The light of a translucent flower.
Shadow on carpet.
A word of thanks.
A smile.
Swifts swooping.
Drips of rain running on a window.
The rooks bashed aside the canes, and cawed at dawn.
Not so bad,
The dreams already broken,
The dawn so bright.

Go too deep and you will drown, warned Seamus Heaney. Yet we must raid the unsaid. Deep, but not into permanent darkness.

⚊⊷⊶⚊

35. LAY-BYS OF THE A12

Lay-by: turnout, aire, pullout, pull-off.

Appended to roads are inlets meant for rest, drivers stretching legs, dropping litter, sipping tea, these days checking messages and mobile maps. Each is unique, a mix of local nature and invasives swirled along the road.

The A12 was formed in 1922. A trunk road to link London's Blackwall Tunnel, right by today's Olympics site, via Essex, Suffolk, and a touch of Norfolk, to arrive at Great Yarmouth by salty Breydon Water. It had been pilgrimage route north to the noisy hospital, now for the last days to the serene cottage unit where care was personal and madly dashed swift by churchyard street.

Under a painter's sky,
High cirrus torn by winds, low scudding cumulus,
Singed charcoal gray along their base,
A project:
Stop at each lay-by.

And so a journey defined by time elapsed became about being and watching. Blue P sign, sharply pull in. A few had much warning and long straights for entrance and departure. Others called for heavy-braking, devilish acceleration into speeding traffic. Danger was central to the method. At some the car was inches from the vehicle river; others had a strip of scrubby meadow.

The first was at flooded marsh, briny far inland, reeds on the fresh dancing in the wind. Above circled a marsh harrier. On a rise was the church assaulted by Cromwell, where ran a black dog fiery and terrible. At the next was a hedge of tinder elms, cracked and spindly, a large oak flipped inside out by wind, a field of rape still green this summer of rain. There was a dog rose, rambling in the hedge, pink and bleached to white the only colors save for the red tin of energy drink. At Darsham, lay-by for slow vehicles to wait at railway crossing, there were clambered rose and sweetbriar of pink and white, cleavers stickily scrambling, shadows dark under thick blackthorn, dense and twisted as it paused between spring spectacle and autumn sloe. There was no birdsong in these lay-by environments, all the natural crushed by internal combustion engine. More bottles were being absorbed by stands of grass.

At North Green were burdock and chrysanthemum garden escapees, banks of wall barley, darts for throwing if only children would come. There was the rushing roar of wheels, false oat grass bobbing, banks of nettle, a single mallow with seams of purple. At the Saxmundham pit stop, flags snapped at the snack caravan. Lorry drivers took tea, van drivers too. In the shadow of an oak, boxes were being moved from one flatbed truck to another, the men pausing, staring. Here was a section of dual carriageway, the central reservation yellow with bold buttercup and white umbels of battered hemlock. Inland was a rippling steppe of barley. At Wickham Market, a hairy landing, yet there were sulfur buttons of lady's bedstraw at the roadside, and ten-foot giant hogweed. A whole hedge of healthy elms, another single mallow. Woodbridge brought more rambling rose, and creamy elder bushes. By the bins was a stand of spear thistle, a sign saying *Litter Please*. On the central reservation were scarlet poppy, the silky petals translucent in the sun. And two foxgloves, nowhere near a woodland edge. At Martlesham meadows was another fast landing, but a wasted stop. A mower had cut and nothing but stems remained. The central reservation, though, was dense with panicles and yellow cat's ear.

A message for the consumption economy: *Reduce Speed Now*, said a sign. No one did.

On the stretch south to the Stour, where the road turned south to follow the valley home, there was a different regime. The central reservation was bare, crumbled concrete, sprayed out with regularities of herbicide.

In this way, stopping helps. American golfer Walter Hagen said, "Don't hurry . . . be sure to smell the flowers along the way."

The next trip, I picked up my son from a station, and as we drove toward the hospital we came upon a brisk cloud shadow exactly at our driving speed. Ahead was the line of the bright sun, and we were in the shade. We were still and yet speeding, unable to escape.

On walking to the town of Tambaichi, Bashō wrote:

Tired and worn
Seeking an inn
I stopped to gaze at wisteria flowering.

36. THE COTTAGE HOSPITAL

Yesterday, my father croaked: "I thought I was going to die last night. All of me stopped working."

We could find no words. Each time we left this hospital, we turned to pass the old house, and ahead was the light of the sun on the sea, the light of the sea in the air, in moisture thrown up by waves. It was breathtaking, not of this world. All was severe and serene, those days. We got the hospital transfer, and this was partly why.

In the garden, there were bulbs of bluebell and alchemilla seedlings to plant. The roses looked good, especially Handel's delicate white, veining a deeper pink each day.

My mother called early. My father had deteriorated. The land was all intense colors. Brilliant blue sky, rich green in hedge, poppy by the roadside, golden barley. It was too late, though I did not yet know it. Parked, walked around the corner by the churchyard, the sun shining, an incandescent light still refracted and reflected by the sea and its spray, swifts slicing silently over the hospital and low down the street.

Inside, the nurse nodded but her eyes were lidded; in front of the ward was a white screen, blocking entry. It slid aside. It was a land of shadow. My mother and brother shook their heads.

Many people today favor the euphemism *passed*, or *passed away*. Neither has much merit. Death carries many taboos. We dare not talk about it, for fear of darkness. Thus do modern rationalists slip into superstitions. We do not speak in case it makes an outcome worse or just more likely. Superstitions are bets on influencing the future. We all seem to do it. Loss of life is an ancient tragedy; the modern one is loss of sense.

Earlier, we did take on taboos. We had to plan for funeral, thanksgiving, cremation, scattering ashes on the water. We hoped he did not mind. It helped us prepare, not making hard decisions when our heads would be scrambled and stomachs cramped and legs gone, and people expressing sympathies and no one knowing what to say.

My father made us laugh. On the final day, my mother, daughter, and I sat around the bed and he said, "I want . . . ," and paused, and we leant forward and said, yes? . . . and he said triumphantly, "a cigarette."

And we laughed. Out loud. And my mother said, "But you gave up in 1962!" And he said with a knowing smile, "I know."

On the wall is one of his watercolors.
And in two thousand homes are others.
Gazed at with fondness and pride.
People thought much of his skill in reading the land.
He left those legacies.

---

37. COME BACK THE WILD

Civilizations come and go; this much we know. But it is curious how little we understand about precisely why they die. Only recently in modern history has the world come to know of the *moai* heads of Rapa Nui, of Mayan temple deep in dense rainforest, of Inca ruin in thin air, of Minoan palace on Crete, of Angkor Wat in Cambodian jungle, each invaded by the wild as soon as people departed.

England's deserted medieval villages are instructive: how easily in future we may come to forget our modern civilization. England's clearances began from the early Middle Ages, and were then forgotten until the mid-twentieth century, when historians and archaeologists led by Maurice Beresford began to search. Despite extensive records for medieval society, historians believed whole village depopulations were rare or only followed the Black Death that slashed the population of Britain in the late 1300s.

At first, Beresford thought there might be a few hundred. After decades of research, he had found more than three thousand—each a village once complete, but then entirely deserted. Beresford wrote how difficult was his research from the late 1940s: "No traveller comes easily to a lost village . . . You must be friends to mud, to green lanes and unused footpaths, to rotting footbridges and broken stiles, to branches and to barbed wire . . . It is so long since anyone wanted to come this way."

What is odd: in seemingly cramped islands, we could so easily have lost even one village. All that remains are earthwork and ridge visible when the sun is low. Some fell in the sea; most were depopulated by grabbing land acts, the commons and villages enclosed, people forced away.

What would happen if we now strolled from city and village? Or just died off? Pavement and walkway would be quickly overrun by grass and flower, which given low nutrient status would mean highly diverse meadows. Expect many orchids.

Existing grasslands and parks would grow tall, then scrub and trees invade. Lawns would take on bramble and birch, becoming scrubby wood within fifteen years. Houses would disappear, like those Mayan ruins. Solar panels would continue to generate electricity, but no one would use it; wind turbines would turn until high gales ripped them apart. Existing woods would darken to dense forest, but some would be eaten out as deer invaded in growing numbers. Many fox would thrive, as would badger. Pond and swimming pool would clog with reed; there would be dragonfly and damselfly. The rivers at low bridges would be blocked with debris, water spilled over banks to create wetlands. Beaver would spread.

There would be no leached nutrients from farm fields, rivers running clear and oligotrophic. Jack pike would become plentiful, growing large. But all the water voles would be eaten by mink, with no controls. American crayfish would complete their invasion. Otters would be present in large numbers, as their top predators today are motorcar and eel trap. Feral pigs from farms would bash down fences and come to town and village forest. Dairy cattle would not survive, nor racehorse. Many domestic dogs would die, but some would join into vicious packs, hunting sheep. Cats would thrive, becoming wilder.

Most buildings would look the same for years, accreting moss and lichen on roofs, plastic window frames holding firm. Those with thatched roofs or weatherboarding would rot and split. Trees would sprout inside. Old glass would shatter. Predatory birds would roost on silent church tower and block of flat; pigeon would decline. Swift would slice the air, swallow and martin dash too, as there would be many insects over a land no longer sprayed. There would be many owls, mice exploding in number as they ate through abandoned houses. Corvids would succeed, clever and adaptable. Rosebay willowherb would quiver pink in wind. There would be dense stands of Japanese knotweed, the riverbank thick with Himalayan balsam, good for bees.

And we would not see any of it.

In AD 400, Rome was a city of 800,000 people, and no writer, painter, or politician imagined its future ruin. A century later, the population was 30,000. "When we contemplate ruins," wrote Christopher Woodward, "we contemplate our own future." In 1855, Richard Deakin catalogued 420 plant species on the Colosseum; now it has been cleaned up to look a proper ruin. Yet check around. There are many contemporary ruins: petrol stations stranded, churches locked, high street shops sucked away by edge-city developments, brutalist blocks, cooling towers.

Monsters await, encouraged as we use up the planet. It could be one against all, and we will become bewildered and stunned, as in the mead hall of the Spear Danes in days gone by, staring aghast, until the greatest place in the world stood empty. We created Grendel, and there is no Beowulf to call upon, no rescue from across the gannet's bath.

And yet now, there was warmth on the evening air, the garden dense with a cloud of determined mayfly. Only this one day do they fly, all heading northeast uphill away from river. They rose over the house and swarmed across the garden. The swallows were content. Then inky rooks beat overhead, balls of young blue and great tit whirring to the feeders. Thyme leaves filled the air with the aroma of hot lands. A young spotted woodpecker chuntered at the feeders. There were orange geum and aquilegia of complex colors and design. Pink and white the bright of parasols, roses tall and thin, metallic purple delphinium. Lupin seemed just hours from flower, everything was agrowth and living and filling this place. Summer had come.

I took a glass of wine amongst the tiger lily fiery and orange. So many other roses too. Some we laid on the oak coffin at the crematorium, back a million years ago. Or was it yesterday? Now the opening line of *L'Étranger* by Camus had become clear. Meursault was not indifferent to his mother's death. He had simply been unhinged, losing all sense of time.

Guessed Philip Larkin in "Going, Going":

> I thought it would last my time . . .

> And that will be England gone,
> The shadows, the meadows, the lanes . . .
> Philip Larkin, 1922–1985

38. ANNIVERSARY

At seven minutes past eight, a skylark appeared. It started singing. It blurred in a hover, the song cascading over chuckling river and banks of tall vegetation. A thrush sang paired clauses from a rowan. The air gently shifted, just a wash and ebb. Willow down floated near-motionless, dropping to cover the wooden bridge and water.

Above the slow flow were pairs of dancing river insects, taking turns to rise as the other fell. The sun was behind cloud, almost out, almost not. The riverbank was home to giants, fifteen-foot burdock, a pink rambling rose over bolted elder, two-meter thistle, the remains of the lockkeeper's garden. Along the path grass was in spectacular flower, the purple and yellow anthers of false oat and cocksfoot all a-froth. All bright colors, yet muted by fogged memory.

The bridge was a good place to write. Now a haze of sunlight held the crumpled leaves of hazel. A little egret flew across the field, white in this green valley not yet scorched by summer. Pairs of black rook flew higher, making their own journeys. Dozens of neon damselfly skipped over water, black roundels on wings an echo of the lockman's pond. Somewhere in this thorn and scrub were the ruins of the cottage and lives long gone. Where ancestors of these birds sang, barges slid past with straining horse, and men cast oyster shell into the water. In those days, no distant sound of car on road, no tarmac at all, no plane above. Just creaking cart and thudding hoof, a distant call fading on the warm breeze.

> Three mallard paddled through the carpet of down,
> Leaving leads of glassy sky.
> Filigree hemlock shivered.
> Leaves sighed, bees buzzed.
> How it was.

The phone rang. It was national radio. An urgent request. But this land was reason to decline. Above and behind, songs of skylark symphony.

JULY

39. VILLAGE EDGELANDS

Do listen. We read how Farley and Roberts rambled among the abandoned roads and routes of the north and west. Each settlement has them: places between boundaries, edgelands not forgotten, just ignored. In the valley, some concepts of montage beauty miss the sparrow and spade, the spaces beside the domestic and farmed. These habitats are not on the itinerary of the tourist bus.

On Harper's Hill, north up the valley flank, is a hidden lay-by. A narrow path cut through twisted hawthorn and young oak, opening to a thin meadow by the turnpike. This day, castles of cumulus towered in the radiant sky. Bee and butterfly hummed and hunted. Cars poured downhill, yet this leached landscape had thirty-six species in flower. Mournful meadow browns chased in packs across stands of yellow agrimony and ribbed melilot, the drifts shimmering in afternoon sun. Agrimony was a wayside perennial in medieval times, used for snakebite and elf shot; melilot was a forage plant, now found in wastes yet dreaming of a field. Signs of another past in this edgeland: a wilder apple red with glossy fruit. It was a meadow good for lying and staring at the sky. Two thrush trilled, more cars rumbled in low gear. An Essex skipper landed on a hemlock, then two damselfly hovered, a neon azure, a gossamer agrion, wing spots blurring in the heat.

Next morning: at the bridge, lower down the same road, the county line, cars clattering. Beneath the river was crystal, flitting with thin shadows of fish. *Beware of the Bull*, warned a long-faded sign, over the fence clambered gold honeysuckle. There are otters, back after excesses of pollution and hunting: the water bloody as hounds bayed and a trumpet played. In later years, a coypu was cornered downriver, those fur-farm escapees iconic and then another heartbreak, officially hunted to extinction.

> Yet this border has become a death trap:
> The spillway is too steep,
> The cars blind,
> The otters slow.

A chaffinch sang in a trembling poplar, stratus trails crisscrossed far above. There were thick crops of bramble and nettle. Further into the Essex side was a blocky building with high windows, locked beyond zinc fence and rusted barbed wire. Such services deep in scrub, pump house and electricity substation. Over grass tussocks, grasshoppers buzzed and floated through the sunlight. More meadow brown dashed over golden ragwort and speedwell. Elder had clambered brick, a pink sweet pea bright among dead elm. Wild and domestic escapees were interwoven.

On the Suffolk side was a splayed wing of sparrowhawk, laid on concrete blocks piled seven high, awaiting deployment. Nearby was a rusting tin of *Pork Luncheon Meat*, long since a food of choice. One day, someone may call it an archaeological remain. More agrion were in rushes by the water, by another pile of shingle a single scarlet hollyhock, swarmed with bee and hoverfly. Upriver was the one black poplar, wet-footed and tall, a wood for clogs and fire-resistant floorboards, for cart brakes and markets long gone.

Private Fishing, warned another sign: *Colchester Angling Preservation Society. Leave No Litter* was their motto, just by a pile of plastic litter and beer cans. This is the local river, but the rights to fish have been taken. The website says there are 1,400 members, seventeen stillwaters, eight miles of river, but a concession: five hundred meters of river are for villagers. There are posed pictures of twenty-pound pike, five-pound chub, roach and dace, gudgeon and perch. The river has an angling language, the swims, streaming stretches for dace, enticing bends, banks for trotting tactics. Ask fishermen, though, and they shake fists at hungry otters.

Back in the village center, there were preparations for a festival and street party. There will be country dancing and hog roast, local food, crowded beer tent. As he walked, Matsuo Bashō saw the plants between the places, but his roads creaked only with carts.

> Long conversations
> Beside blooming irises—
> Joys of life on the road.
> > Matsuo Bashō,
> > 1644–1694

⬿⬾

40. NATURE AT A NUCLEAR POWER STATION

Many at Suffolk's coast are drawn to the regency charm of Southwold and Aldeburgh, the wildlife of Minsmere and Dunwich Heath. From each, you can see a far white dome and neighboring gray block. Many pretend these are not visible; Sebald stumbled on furzy heath looking and not-looking. Once a fishing village sprawled by rabbit warren and clipped dune, a remote smugglers' spot, Sizewell has been known for fifty years for the hint of nuclear fear. In a box, somewhere, is super 8 film fading to bleached yellow and orange. There we were, playing on the sandy beach by lapping waves as cranes clustered at the Magnox box. In a folder are later images of Chernobyl's Reactor 4 and galloping gamma ray detector, and the wild surprise of the exclusion zone.

Next-generation nuclear may come here too, after the wind farm far to sea. A corner of woodland was taken for the wind substation. In meadow, woodland belt, marsh, stream, and shingly shore are orchid and otter, hobby and goshawk, bog bean and red deer, kittiwake and buzzard. The energy company received seven hundred hectares when public ownership became private. This is their best nature reserve. One day when a growling thunderstorm had raced across the coast and left behind blue sky and friendly cumulus, we walked the many habitats.

"Once they've found us, people do like to return," said Carl Powell of Suffolk Wildlife Trust, smiling. Out here marshy children were born with webbed feet, half mermaid and half fairy, splashy indigenes where the ague gripped and smugglers for centuries stitched their routes over ligger boards and sea lavender beds. Between cliff and marsh, Sizewell Gap was good for landing tea and tobacco, gin and coffee, run inland to the Hadleigh gang. It was a foggy trade, thousands of gallons in single shipments. Every rural parish had its gin and tea shop; captured contraband was auctioned off by the border force and reentered the economy. Now we drive to the supermarket, the trade routes just as global.

We passed plantations of tall pine on Kenton Hills, found hawker dragonfly at a fire pond. Sizewell Belts graded to old marsh, distant beefs grazing bright meadow. Pollarded willow lined the dikes where water vole had returned; a family of swan hissed. We walked over acid grassland and back into Rackham Pits: trees have grown over depressions once used for washing imported sisal. A herd of three hundred red deer roam, and by an ancient silver birch four meters in circumference was their churned meeting ground. The trees gave way again to marsh and meadow. A good time would be June for carpets of common spotted and southern marsh orchid amongst pink of ragged robin. But, still, this would do. Though there are plans, government hesitates long, using up fossil fuels more, hoping that fracking would deliver cheap gas instead. And still destroy this all.

On the far side of the wet meadow the containment dome gleamed above the trees. The wide beach of sand dune and shingle bank led to the churning sea, warmed by the station outfall, a flock of squealing kittiwake nesting above the waters rich with fish. Even at the power station, there was little forbidden ground. None of the foreshore, dune, or beach was enclosed; all remain a relic of England's commons. In this way do the ancient and modern coexist.

41. DIGGING FOR VICTORY

On the borderlands of each village and town, by dusty road and racing railway track, under power lines or etched between house and hedge, lie the farmlets of Albion. Remnants of savage Enclosure Acts of the 1700s and 1800s, three thousand times elected government stealing away the commons, these parcels becoming the jumbled allotments and guinea gardens that waxed and waned, and became popular again.

In the Second World War, allotments were vital for the Dig for Victory campaign, swelling in number to 2 million. The ministry printed pamphlets on growing the exotic potato, the carrot and onion, encouraged the formation of pig clubs. Vegetable rows appeared on bomb plot, front garden, village green, rail line side strip, and airfield. Postwar they fell away. Big agriculture rumbled up, people had other priorities, rationing ended. The 1960s' Thorp inquiry called for rules to erase the tatty huts and irregular design, said they should be called leisure gardens. Government surprisingly said no, dug in heels, but did nothing to stop the decline. Developers and planners were the new enclosers. Today, some 300,000 plots remain.

Up a dim lane overhung with ivy, by a field with rolled-up bales, the village allotments were a mix of design and wild chaos. Squash and maize, potato and sweet pea, raspberry cane over black plastic, riotous weed and waspy wildflower. One patch was all poppy and mallow, swaying red and purple in the warm breeze. Every shed was different, every compost pile. There was incinerator and stacked tool, raised bed awaiting the spade and fork. Shiny CDs spun from bamboo poles to ward off birds; there was tall artichoke, wispy fennel, onion in razor rows, a snapping flag.

> An axe handle was propped against a hut.
> It was seasoned, chiseled from a tree, aging with wind and rain.
> This was to stray into another century,
> When digging was good.

Allotments have always been political spaces, statements of personal intent regarding the food system and local land identity. What emerges is what people want, then paths diverge. What the country needs is more of this. More digging, more fitness, less fatness. Allotments stimulate metaphors about the way we live, wrote Colin Ward, about storing produce, looking after the earth and friendships, about self-reliance, planning for the future.

From across the meadow came a keening cry. A pigeon powered past. With stiff wing beats, a sparrowhawk dashed faster and both were gone.

Between the allotments and the Fen, the rilled common between village and river, was Little Lye, Andora's patch of wildflower meadow. The bee orchids have been mapped and marked over the years, but this summer was too dry. The soil was cracked; there were many butterfly. The meadow had become stands of golden St. John's wort and the pioneering pink of rosebay willowherb, the fireweed of city bomb plot, rare until railways punched corridors across the country, their downy seeds following. By a sheet of corrugated iron was a sudden movement, a huge toad scurrying in the dust of rabbit diggings. Too many rabbits, too few orchids.

I gave a copy of Kunitz's earthy book on gardening and being, *The Wild Braid*, to Ronnie Blythe. He wrote a handwritten letter. "What a thoughtful book, a contemplation of being old and being in the garden. It is beautiful . . . I used to visit Cedric Morris at Hadleigh when he was ancient and blind, lying in the sun in his garden where his exotics, the plants he had brought to Suffolk from the Mediterranean, had become a kind of glamorous hayfield. But I will be mowing the lawn this hot afternoon and, like Kunitz, be half lost in daydreams." In a garden pot dreams one of Morris's pink geraniums.

Other hopes have been dashed, and we can do nothing. One of the Assington elms has gone under. All its leaves were cooked. The horse chestnut leaf miner came, trees racing to autumn color. They had looked in better shape, the hot spring held back the pest, gave the trees advantage. But year on year, damage accumulates.

Those with gardens will keep digging,
Scimitar swifts scissoring the sky.
Dim down here,
Blackbird chipping alarm calls,
Gray dunnock hopping in the underworld.

—⦁⦁⦁—

42. UNDER ANOTHER ATOMIC SKY

Dark was the horizon under hard clouds, fishing boats and yachts bobbing on the mercury river. The air was temporarily stilled, a windsurfer becalmed. It was three hours to high tide, the clinker-built ferry down concrete steps. When the castle was built by the second Henry, this was a seaport. Now the spit is a dozen miles long, the village of Orford itself stranded far from the treacherous reach at Shingle Street. We had been driving along the bottom of the sea, thunder crashing, the air as wet as the land, just as it had been two days previously as we converged on the small church for the funeral.

Earlier we had laughed. We needed to, after sitting with the funeral director. "I was a dairy farmer," he said, reassuringly holding out his gnarled hands. We all need someone to manage the gate. Cremation began in Europe in the 1860s, and now only three of ten British dead are buried. At the green crematorium when the dairyman led the cortege, his hands clasped, there were three roses on the coffin.

The funeral morning was filthy. Rain lashed, the ground underwater, stomachs knotted. For successive nights, the same ghoul chased through dreams, a tangled ball of twisting shadow, fearful wraith grasping. It caught me on the stairs of a theater; it caught me running up a hill; it caught me on a battlefield. None of these were known places in this world. Reydon church was full, standing room only. Yet as the service ended the layer of cloud rolled away, the sun pouring from a fresh sky. Under the wooden roof were lancing sunbeam and the rising song of Vaughan Williams's *The Lark Ascending*. Carpenter Tim Barr had fashioned small squares of beech, my father's favorite wood, one for each guest. In the Church Room was food and drink.

In the middle of madness, the world does not stop. It takes no notice at all. Some 600,000 people a year die in the UK, touching relatives and friends of about a third of the population. Yet it feels we have become less familiar with death, as it migrates from infants, who survive better, to the elderly, who live longer but are more lonely.

This day, we escaped the storm, and watched it advance again. The Ness is a stretched spit of shingle ridges, bright with yellow-horned poppy, red valerian, quivering mats of acid sea campion, sea kale clumps. Ninety-nine years ago the War Department took it for their tests, far they hoped from the curious eye. Here jumped the first man from a plane with parachute, here too the development of radar, Barnes Wallis's bouncing bomb, later stress-testing of nuclear weapons in the six shingle-submerged laboratories. At the Cold War deeps, six hundred servicemen and women were stationed on The Ness. The RAF gave a daily rum ration: a harsh posting, it was, out at the Suffolk coast.

We walked across the fresh marsh, grass and rush swaying in the beating wind. Birds were down, huddled on the scrape.

Oyster catcher wheeped.
Avocet tottered.
Soft stonecrop lined the path.
The agitated sea was a mile distant,
Yet silent.
The breath between sky and land was gone behind a wall of rain,
The world toppled fast.

At the bailey bridge, marsh fresh-green merged to salt, smudged with mauve of sea lavender, and then sharply to shingle, glistening brown and rust, tones of toffee, pink, violet, charcoal, and pearl. Rain pounded the open spit. The lighthouse disappeared beyond the pewter curtain, the columned pagodas too. Sky sounds and bouncing rain leached clear away the noise of the mind.

South awaited sculptures, a performance of jazz and the sounds of nature and human intertwined, where intention and lie, myth and truth, swirl through every story. There were craters, decades after bombs were cast from the sky, on steep sides protrusions of shell and twisted wire, lichens long-lived. Still rain fell, thunder grumbled, crashing over death barrows piled high with shingle. Inside, pale paint peeled from walls, flecks floating on the puddles. Drips plinked and echoed in abandoned corridors, moss wet and green on fallen ducts. Abandoned instrument panels were disconnected, the cable innards butchered from walls of green. A whole form of civilization had departed. On the roofs of two pagodas were colonies of herring gull, yowling at human reinvasion. They too were recent arrivals, stopping to nest only after the military had packed their bags.

The concerto was in the concrete armory, an arched dark space. We huddled wet inside the dripping glacier, the words of Rob Macfarlane's libretto and Arnie Somogyi's composition, the sounds of bird and fishman calling, of scientist and birder, crunching shingle and waves that ever came. Then blew in the sun, and we stepped into a landscape bright with cumulus. The tide was retreating, and we walked and walked, warming in the tearoom overlooking sailboats and blue water. We had lifted some stones, saw the skin and bones. The world was no longer the same place.

Another Wanderer was Johnny Cash:

> I went out walking under an atomic sky
> Where the ground won't turn and the rain it burns
> Like the tears when I said goodbye . . .
>
> I went wandering.

Bono, 1960–

43. HEAT WAVE

The valley was glorious, a tapestry of drought. Lawns had gone over. A clear spring bubbled from a hillside road, where it always had, always frozen on winter mornings. Drivers seemed maddened, roaring through the gears, in a hurry to end it all. Poppy were dying, yet barley ready, wheat gray-green still. Some roads have been cheaply repaired patch by plastered patch. Soon they will split and go over again. In evening, cool air leaked into the kitchen, a moth outside daring to dance.

It had been the hottest day for seven years.
Taste of humid heat of forests where leaches fix on legs.
Here fiery, just fewer parasites.

An insistent wren, nothing more.
After sunset, a dusty wind blew in the trees,
Buzzing cockchafer beetles clattered close.
A silent bat quartered.
A horse huffed.
The moth rose slowly.
The bat turned.

The desert heat built all next day, then came dark matter. A green storm appeared out west, and in came lightning and hissing rain. Daylight fled. By evening, in the pale salmon light, it was cool outside but hot in, the windows open and the air dense. A woodpecker chuntered from far. The sky flared orange in the altostratus. Entire events seemed possible, even likely.

The next day, an early appointment with television crew and presenter on the cliffs. Can you talk about coastal erosion: I knew the place. They drew up at the church. The street with no houses led to the sandstone cliffs. The morning sun was low over the calm sea, the meadow swarmed with bee and butterfly, yellow beach below, orange cliff, luminous crunching waves, silvered sky to east and blue behind. Swallows swerved in updrafts and stalled. The camera rolled yet the world had been stunned. Out to sea, the drowned fishing village. To the south, out to sea too, Easton meadows and war black birds: Flying Fortress, Lancaster, Halifax, swirling up to lumber away and open bomb doors on the guilty and gilded, limping back gushing smoke. Over these same cliffs, on days when the dawn sun shone on a troubled world, watchers held their breath.

Lie back, see the trembling flowers on the sea breeze,
White aster,
Clover,
Corn cockle;
Watch honeybee and slumber to the crackle of heat.

AUGUST

44. PAUSE FOR RAGWORT

In sulfured summer, a farming pause. Soon the stutter, and engine roar. It will be the day and the night of the harvester. Once dusty cereal fields swarmed with calling farmworkers, children beating for fleeing rabbit, families all laid in hedgerow for bait of bread and cold tea, perhaps beer and fatty pork. Now above farmyard and village street swallows slide and tear targets from the clean air, the evenings flickering with bats. After a point, there is nothing more to do but wait. The last tawny softly hooted. Oilseed rape was in, fields prickly with lime-green stalk and shard of seedpod by hedge and road. Flocks of pigeon roamed. Next would be barley, later wheat, browbeaten by black mildew. Early harvests from the south were poor.

> One field in the valley
> Was dotted with ragged roundels.
> In crashed storm and warm rain,
> The combines crept back to dark lairs.

Meanwhile, it had been a splendid summer for ragwort. Who would be a farmer? This bright Compositae is related to chamomile and feverfew, medicinal and good plants. Golden ragwort thrives in tired arable fields, neglected meadow, wayside verge. It is a notifiable weed, toxic, a bad plant. The ministry has a Ragwort Code: all landowners, you must cut or spray or pull. All ragwort must go. Myths are many: it is horse slayer, cattle killer, symbol of farming decay. A company selling a removal tool claimed ragwort was annually responsible for six thousand horse deaths. The ministry points to thirteen. In the Netherlands, where *Senecio* also spreads, a postmortem system has yet to find a case of poisoned horse. Given choice, horses do not consume. It grows untouched in meadows.

Official weed or not, preferred extinction creates a problem. It is pollen for butterfly, moth, bee, and beetle. Thirty species of insect depend exclusively on ragwort, another twenty-two eat much in their diet. Thus, kill or leave? Green or dry, it causes fatal cirrhosis of the liver. Put on gloves if you are going to pull it, never let it in hay as animals will eat the lot. Essex Wildlife Trust is a landowner with a plan: ragwort is left for insects, but managed when too common. They cut, spray, pull, and pause.

The poet John Clare rambled far, half-maddened by places and plants lost and loved, calling ragwort a humble flower with tattered leaves, littered gold, creating a "sun tanned sward in splendid hues."

———⟊⟊⟊ꟾ⟊⟊⟊———

45. THE END OF THE ROAD

At all times, Suffolk had three seaside habitats: shingle, sand dune, sandstone cliff. The shingles drift, sand dunes accrete, cliffs crumble. To reach the sea, you must travel arterial roads to settlements at the rim. In heavy rain pouring from sou'westerlies, after walking Halvergate's soggy swamp with marshman Billy Frosdick: there was Covehithe, reeling on cliffs rich with herringbone gravels. In the medieval era, it was a thriving fishing village; all that remains is a lime-washed farm and yard, a stranded pair of cottages, the flinty double church.

The narrow lane was hedged with sloe blackthorn, twisted and long-sculpted by racing wind. Bracken fronds shone by purple mallow. The sky was in the puddles. The cloudy veil was low and dark, all the pigs were in their arks. Just as the line on maps disappears into the sea were signs: *Danger, No Public Right of Way.* And routes off to either side, where walkers stray. To the north, the wheat was in; beyond the church tower loomed high. Far below, yeasty waves grumbled at the shore. Where wheat was sown last autumn, where great machines had roared, the field was tipping over. Lines of crop fell into thin air. There were losses here, land and memory, house and harbor, cottage garden. All under the frothy sea.

Five hundred meters have gone this past century. With the saturation of soil, there was likely more falling soon. To the north was Benacre, a single oak trunk standing in the sea, the last tree of Doggerland's great forest, now under the foaming deeps.

To the south, Easton Bavents, once a mile and half to sea, the church and thronging markets gone. Julian Tennyson, great-grandson of the poet, wrote in *Suffolk Scene* that Easton Broad was "one of the quietest and most deserted places in Suffolk." It had become so, by the 1930s. But then came the war, and he died in Burma. Old maps show that where the shore protrudes to sea, then longshore drift and tides will loathe it. Nesses have been sheared away. Kirby wrote on his 1736 map at Easton, *the ruines of a church near this place devoured by the sea.* Wrote Crabbe of this coast, "With ceaseless motion comes and goes the tide." The ebb tide flows north, the flood south: this is why fishermen told of steaming down to the Shetlands and up to Dover. At home is a piece of bog oak dredged from here, dark and dense as iron.

> This porous place of dreams,
> Of comings and goings.
> Water washing out and in.
> Light from sun and sea,
> Advancing on land at every dawn.

Beyond the wheaty tops, a half kilometer inland was the church raised within the ruins of the greater original. The parish in the late 1600s could not survive the falling tithes, the community going into the sea, and wrecked it to build a tiny one inside. The outer ruins were decorated with knapped flint, sliced in squares and fine arches. From high in sky, sandstone gargoyles have since stared down on grassy graves. There were nettles in the nave, ivy swarming over walls, flints crusty with white lichen. Inside the church, *Pleurococcus* greened the wet west wall. A plaque named forty-two Covehithe men serving in the army and navy during the Great War.

In this place was born Bilious Bale, loud bishop under Edward VI, confidant to Thomas Cranmer. Yet who today will save these coastal places in the face of storms and sea rise; who will persuade us all to live differently to prevent the climate from changing more?

> Without some shouting,
> It could well be the end of the road.

—⚒—

46. NIGHTWALK

The sun was setting inland, our intention to walk the coast, from the eastern-most point of Britain south to the other surviving town along this stretch. That August evening, Lowestoft itself seemed abandoned. The North Denes was a caravan site, once the fishermen's beach village of pebble-built cottages, red-roofed curing sheds, fish yards and pickling plots. The location less far back of shouted PE lessons, cross-country runs through ice and water between the net spars. At Ness Point, concrete war defenses were broken at the shore, waders picking for insects. Here the fish boys tanned their ganseys, fashioned by women who knitted as they walked. A few miles north, Yarmouth jerseys were blue. The greatest rivals are always the nearest, both needed to look different. We stopped to remember a night, decades ago.

It had been a dream summer of all childhoods. The sun shone from dawn to dusk. Drought was widespread. The last days of school echoed to bounce of basketball, visits to the local pub. We dissected the last rat, hand-drew irises, were released to study all those hot days. On the day of the final exam, a botany practical, we played those staff at basketball, winning comfortably, records a smiling entry in my diary. The beach drew us in, forming gritty backdrop to a salty summer. Sunday was duty as canoe lifeguards. We painted the hut, as we had previous summers, and canoed in the waves. We raced seals and warned swimmers of hidden danger. Onshore breeze whipped up waves around those then solid sea defenses and graspy tank traps.

On the night of the third of July, after working the airless bar at the holiday camp, friends met at midnight by the War Memorial. We walked down narrow cliff score, and set a beach fire that crackled bright through the short night. It was to be American Bicentennial Day, a handy excuse.

> We had crates of beer and food,
> And swam in phosphorescence,
> Pushing out the northern lights of sea.
> We rose out of the water green as ghosts.
> The sun leapt from the sea.
> We clinked bottles and laughed.

Now all was bleaker. We were older, the economy had bled and stumbled. Fences hemmed cavernous warehouses, empty save for oil stain and peeling wall. By fish market leaking rust and fenced-in too was the row of bethels and places of worship, right where fishermen stumbled ashore with pockets of pay in search for someone, more likely some pub, to save their soul. Half the country's herring was landed here.

A century ago, half a thousand drifters and trawlers packed this harbor. Now there were six. Smokers stood outside the bingo hall, praying for salvation, knowing the house always wins. Bingo replaces fishermen, and some call this progress.

The light leached from the sky, inland dark clouds beginning to shiver with lightning. On the wide sands of South Beach, three children bounced at the promenade, one shouting back with city accent, "Dad, Dad, are we allowed on the sand?"

> The beach was empty.
> We smiled,
> And so did he,
> Waving yes,
> Go on.

At Pakefield the Jolly Sailors beckoned, where the roaring boys drank their beer. We walked up the cliff, sat outside, looking at the sea. Waves advanced, crumped, retreated, came again. We waited until almost dark, then advanced ourselves. High tide was due at 2:18 AM, there were promontories to skirt. At the shore church, gravestones stood dark against the dim of western sky. Lightning flashed in far clouds. Amid the Kessingland dunes were clinker-built boat and rusty capstan, and we walked into darkness. On the cliff top was the holiday camp at the Grange, the house with a view held by Rider Haggard for forty-five years, where often stayed Kipling to write of smuggling romance. The waning moon was due at sea, but cloud cover was complete.

We walked in and out of miles more dune and shingle. The tall sandstone and gravel cliffs were dark, could be foreboding, except we could imagine the tops: by day, yarrow meadow and bumblebee, swallow swatting insects on the updrafts. At night, all was different. There were percolation ponds to pass, brackish at the edge of the land, leaking fresh water under the sand and topped by salt on the highest tide. All was quiet, just pinking redshank. Far ahead was a strip of glittering jewels in the darkness. We walked towards the town at a moderate pace, just on the middle way between wild cliffs and whispering waves.

Blink. The town disappeared. It was midnight and Southwold streetlights had switched off.

The lighthouse glowed red and white occulting beams, marking sandbanks and the coast itself. The town was still there.

It grew darker as clouds lifted. To the west inland, stars appeared and advanced east. We passed silver birch trunks cast on the shore, scattered from cliffs above. Covehithe's tower was solid against the starry sky. Waves thumped at the shore, a luminous line to our left. Suddenly the clouds had gone.

The moon rose. All was bright with silvered shine. Shadows were strong. We had to sit awhile at Easton Broad, watching the shimmering path of light stretched to the horizon's heaven. The world had come to a halt. This was a dream worth inhabiting. Waves, moonlight, and souls abandoned on the shore.

There were also biting mosquito and sandhopper. We levered up and stood on sore feet, knees creaking, backs aching from soft shingle. Yet there were no nagging thoughts. Just the invisible town ahead, the ground beneath our feet. And the silver channel to the moon above the mighty waters. We walked past Peter Boggis's cliffs and lands, another house on the tops about to go over. It was on these cliffs that our father grew up in a railway carriage and played with Peter and the other cousins. Skylark flew over the meadows, became fixed in their lives, and then ours too.

High tide came, splashing at the tightest cliff. The tide had taken the hard sand, and we tramped through deep shingle, toward dark streets, past the pier, strolling up through the town to our mother's house, all the radiant thoroughfares lit by moonshine. We wondered why this does not happen more—the walking, the switching off. How places change when artificial light ceases to dominate.

> The night air was a new flavor,
> Musty and organic,
> Mixed with tang of burned fuel.

We quietly started cars, heading south and west. Days and nights had passed, yet we had walked for only six hours. At the reed beds, a barn owl rushed from the trees and flew on. Later in the valley, a badger leapt from a hedge and trotted in the headlamps, on its own nightwalk. A line of light formed low on the eastern horizon.

> Sometimes walking is better than dreaming.

―━ⱱ⬧ⱱ━―

47. SOON, THE DEPARTURE

It was October, cool night and cold morning, and yet it was August. The flowers were bright, the pots needed regular water. The forecast was for more dry days but chill winds. Then it rained one evening and through the night hours. Rise, they said, for the sky will shine. At four o'clock, there was a high conjunction of Venus and Jupiter, the planets combining as one bright star. The sky dome was clear, a lower line of gray cloud to the east.

> It was the time of year to stare at Cassiopeia,
> To wish the Pleiades would burst with shooting stars.
> Planes blinked.
> Sheep bleated.
> Nothing else.

At work was the roller coaster of recruitment, dog days on the calendar but turning into a record year. The bomber command board, long discussions, changing policy as data updated. Map captains pored over numbers, cheered by conclusions.

Back in the slow vale, the land slouched. The western sun was low, the light brilliant, the mosaic fields green, yellow, dusty brown. A tractor stacked straw as we walked, sheep murmuring. The roadside oak and ash both were bold and sturdy. Wissington church was cool, the medieval dragon on the old stone wall snarling yet stilled. It was dark and dusty inside; outside the sun glittered in the grass at the gravestones. There were small potatoes in reject piles at the side of harvested fields, in the coverts bitter blackberry. The scent of harvested field, the sweet organic dust, filled the valley. It was a grand moment of the year, when food flows from the land. Yet it was also a wistful time. Soon swift will drift and swallow gather on the wires.

The garden and pots still were bright, but autumn awaited. It was darker earlier. Would there be heat again? Between sky and land, under cloud and over golden field, the stretched long life of hope. Could we find a way to protect this, to breathe and sleep and breathe again? In the middle of things, a fruit fly circled, a spindly spider waited. A giant ground beetle crawled across the kitchen floor, twice the size of any seen before.

Once upon a time,
The garden was quiet and sheep content,
The sky utterly silent under glittering stars.
Soon night would be over and dreams forgotten.
The windows were wide,
The night air fresh and beckoning.
Limbs might be of iron,
The clock ringing.
Or it may be dark and the night long yet.
Only in daylight do the hours dash by.

Clear sky. A young tawny screeched, one, two, three times. A mother owl burbled gently. All else was quiet. The international space station hummed over between star dome and trails of planes. The night air was scented too, with thyme and lavender. Then at two in the morning, standing by the windows dark and quiet, an explosion of streaks, the dark sky torn by fire and flame.

Some valley fields so golden with grain were now brown, the turned sod and silvered plow. Hot air was pushed up in a vortex and anvil clouds towered black and menacing. The light of late day turned green, rolling waves of sound crashing along the valley. Rain poured through streets. The house shook under the onslaught, artillery thumping, washing the dust away forever. In the morning, the valley was still full of storm, the rain inside the clouds and the road a river. It was a good day for reading, gazing at the garden through glass.

When the sun broke through, the swifts had gone.
The valley was washed with warmth and orange light.
Not for another year those sweeping scythes,
Those gulping birds,
Those midge-enemies.
They were here; the next day an aching absence,
An empty sky.

⟞⟞⟋⟍⟝⟝

48. THE TINKER'S COTTAGE

Every marsh has an abandoned cottage. On one was the Tinker's, submerged under bramble crop and elder snaked through window frames, the roof frail and plum in the garden gone wild and long. It was the finest place, views north to the Blyth and Bulcamp on the far side. The sea breeze was active and salty, the stunning sun in a clear sky. Inside a silent spell had been cast on the last lives that once were here. An armchair sprouted springs, the kitchen chimney split with rust. Many tins spilled from cupboards where shelf spars had fallen far. There was an iron iron, a curved knife, hooks on the beams for hanging hams. The stairs were rotten and gone to pieces. A gas bottle in the kitchen corroded danger. In the wrecked front room, a grand piano had creased under folded ceiling.

We felt we could take this place. Build a fine veranda for views of marsh and town beyond, where sparkled the ozone blue of sea. Upriver we would see past pines to Blythburgh and the church tower in the reeds. But all that would happen was decay, more subsidence, memories leached away. When the kitchen was warm and bread in the oven, it would have felt bitterly remote in pitiless winters, floods lapping at the door; it would still have been parched in burning summers, long walks for drinking water. Foods from marsh and river, but never enough to feed well. But then again, there was a piano.

By the river wall shimmered with mauve sea lavender, sticks and posts in the mudflats awaited landscape painters. A drainage mill capped with aluminum stood on the far bank. Little and great egret lifted slowly, also a pair of laboring heron, crying crankily. Greylag geese stamped through the scrapes and above dropped flashing lapwing.

The trail was east. Just before the dog farm was the route of the narrow-gauge railway, fifty years a success and closed in 1929, driven by an engineer who lived in Southwold and held Chinese fancy-dress parties. Enthusiasts have tried to relaunch, but to no avail. At the farm were pheasant pens and kennels for terriers. Swallow chittered through the dense flies of farmyard. We walked past coverts and disused pits, ancient barrows crammed with dead, through bracken stands and over sheep land of acid grass.

> A partridge was in the fescue,
> The spectacled yellow around its eye
> Perfectly sad.
> It did not rise,
> Tipping its head as we hove close.
> Over the reeds loomed dark harriers.

In a cool copse of oak and sweet chestnut was great silence. We stood stiffly in the shadow, dragonfly darting in the dappled altar light. At the wood exit was the taste of salt, the bright breeze of coast and its wildness of reeds. The wind was inside the land, the rush and susurrus, shush and hush again, a rippling wet-grass prairie by the sea, on constant move yet never leaving.

Near Dingle Great Hill, two meters high, the reed line ceased at heaped shingle. Waves were rushing at the sandy shore. In the glittering light of the middle sea was a single sail. It seemed quite still, yet moments later had displaced far. We had to sit down, the light so stunning it disconnected the brain. In the distance to the south was the power station, to the north the fretted harbor wall. We had to sit and watch the sea. After a while it was still the sea. Nearby shingle was fenced for nesting sea swallows. Pebbles at the shore glistened wet as the finest polished jewelry.

North was a dead porpoise. The carcass was red as rust, beak prominent, eyes blank, the body horribly scarred. Inland the village was noisy with visitors search-ing for an aim in life. We trod the north bank of Blackshore back to silence, and crossed the bailey bridge. Even before the financial crunch, the Environment Agency announced it would not repair sea defenses along the river. Indifferent or penniless, the effect would be the same. One sky-blue cottage was once Don and Rene Horwood's, where they watched the tide rise in fifty-three, flow in front door and out back, later the sea crashing through the weak seawalls. It has become too easy to forget the power of an angry sea.

On the sunlit terrace of the Harbour Inn, the tinker's local, overlooking the rippling plain and gorsey slopes, was beer from the town brewery, porcelain plates of fish and chips. We could breathe deeply. Time was passing, it would get easier.

<hr />

49. THE TURN

And thus, the summer that rarely seemed to sparkle had turned, the tapestry of fields white under waves of gulls. Tractors rumbled, the fields brown, barns full, gas grain dryers pouring energy into food. There have been two years of poor yields, dry spring/wet summer, then cold spring/hot summer. Neither good. These years of recession have brought gleaners to the valley, men and women with plastic bags, hiding faces, collecting onion and potato discards. Now an experiment: some stubbles have not been plowed, long-nosed tractors direct seeding into the soil. Minimum tillage had come, could lock long-term carbon in the soil and reduce water erosion. More rain fell, gales sweeping leaves from birch and poplar. The roads under rusted horse chestnut were a rash of crushed conkers.

For two days last week, clear skies brought crystal sunlight, and to the west late in the day, the varnished grass and bracken fronds shone and quivered in the east wind. Stands of wild carrot bobbed white and pink, and *Agrostis* panicles bur-nished with a thousand suns. Rooks cawed homeward arrival, speaking of fresh furrow and pasture probed. Then came a cackling green woodpecker, swooping along hedge boundary, and far above, the first echelon of geese down from the Arctic. Sheep were now in the long grass of the neighboring meadow, contented murmurs seeping into the house in the early hours.

The land shrank, the valley closing to the width of a field. Lightning flashed as the storm advanced, a tropical hue to the air.

> The sky was on the road,
> The swallows flying low.
> Eighty trawled around the house at early morning.
> The youngsters stuttered,
> Part hovered,
> Fell and flew.

The adults dipped wings and simply swerved, letting air do the work. The whole flock turned together in the sunlight, was gone from this world. The air rippled and all the birds were flowing across the sky, slightly displaced, dark swooping again.

Many were the mosquito bites, acquired from *tomillares* of resinous pine and rosemary, lavender and thyme, dwarf Kermes oaks and aniseed fennel, where buzzed grasshoppers and at night the waxing moon hanging over water. There dashed swifts over the terra-cotta tiles and white sails on the cobalt sea.

Here in the valley, many are the swallows over barnyards with horse and cattle, none at all at farms with only corn. Livestock and their flies fetch the swallows, as do gardeners. At some moment those birds will sail south. There should be a ceremony. We could line the roads and salute, bid farewell. But they will silent slip away, those determined migrators, the village abandoned once again.

SEPTEMBER

50. THE PATH

I daresay you have heard of gritty urban walks to football grounds. One is the wildest of the professional leagues. First-generation stadiums were raised a century ago in industrial heartlands and expanding suburbs. Lately a new migration, relocations to town edges, changing supporters' travel patterns. This blue-and-white one is on the northern limits of the first Roman capital, and now we park on village street and walk a mile up green lane, across fields, over bypass bridge, joining others strolling up from the town itself.

Mist was in the valley. A groggy swallow swerved by a tribe of starling. The gray gutters were filled with crushed acorn and beech mast. A sallow man in singlet sat by tall grass in front garden, beer in hand, the lawnmower defeated. A small boy ran circles in the pale sun, waving his arms at greenfly. The hillside lane was flanked with hedge elm and blackthorn sloe, a white horse padded across a paddock. Two animals shave the land: horse and outdoor pig. In the time of the draft horse that stumbled and nodded, they rarely grazed, the land too precious.

The mildewed wheat had been plowed. Beyond the shaky stile, the old right of way angled from field edge to far corner. Each year walkers tramp a route through stubble or young wheat, beans, rape. Now, the dusty field was harrowed down, a path emerging as feet scuffed up regolith. It skirted the top of the embankment, where traffic was becalmed, drivers staring blankly. The slope was dense with yellowing maple, yet a shredded lorry tire had spun to the top. Under sycamore with fungal tar spot were excavations of badger. A sunken lane switched back to the bridge, was dark and silent. The crowd called for a sermon, a lesson for life, for once not disappointed. On return, the stamped path was clearer. Last year, it had a wandering kink, first trod under evening moonlight. Everyone follows the path, and so it stays, until the plow returns. Footpaths were once peopled, places to walk and talk. Ronnie Blythe has written of country paths thronged with men, women, and children walking to work, to see friends, to church, to the shops.

Next morning,
Webs of garden spiders dripped with dew.
The air barely moved yet tugged at silver silk.
The webs had twenty-one or twenty-two radial strands.
At each hub was a tan spider darkly striped.
Yet their time was done.
A web collapsed in whirr of wings,
Folding away.

Blue and great tit continued swooping to the feeders. In nearby Assington a dozen cars were parked at the village hall, the teams ready for ritual, rubbing hands, stamping boots. Thirty thousand teams play football weekly. At the flinty church where sheep had gathered under parkland trees, there were few cars. In days gone by, religion was equipment for coping with endless poverty, the ceaseless lack of hope. Now pews are mostly empty.

In the garden, butterfly flitted over buddleia, the whole valley filled with the kitchen scent of onion harvest.

---

51. MUD BIRDS

Westerly gales brought drenching rain. Dregs blew over mid-morning, the coast calling. In the mid-nineties, holes were punched in a seawall that for a thousand years had protected dry fields of Essex, and crop evolved to salt marsh. Tollesbury is famed for its fisher-sailors who raced the marshy tides and crewed America's Cups. A red lightship was tethered to the olive marsh. On the far side was a decommissioned nuclear station, beyond Baker's peregrine-haunted lands of the Dengie.

A paved lane passed by sewage works, and quartering the sticky field, just twenty feet away, was a buzzard, coverts the color of cloud. It hunted the margins of farmland and salt. The horizon was rimmed by a bowl of hills, church towers rising from inland trees, to the northeast was Mersea Island and its mast forest down on the front. In the Essex archipelago, islands shimmer offshore, ships neither arriving nor departing, culturally apart too. You are always on Mersea, on Canvey, never in.

There was the tang of sea on the crumbling seawall, warbling waders and warmth of sun. Marsh samphire was clumped in flower, by mauve banks of sea lavender and green glasswort. At the wall terminus was a cushion of grass, water dashing on the ebb tide. The fastest person in the world can swim at five miles per hour, tidal water is faster. It looked safe but was not.

Settling into the land, the birds gathered. "The saltings," said Samuel Bensusan, author of five hundred marshland stories, "where the air was musical." Gulls squealed, a curlew curved upwind. It skimmed the shiny mud, a rising warbling call cleaving autumn air. Three sentinels of the marsh flashed over the wall, racing up-creek with teu-eus. Then came sandpiper. Twenty appeared over the saltings, banked high, turned in the pale sunlight, dropped to the mudflats. The tide fell, a foot then two, more waders came to contented piping. Soon a thousand had flown in; glued to the flat shore all turned to face the wind.

The slick sediment looked innocuous, blue mud, silver mud, brown and green mud. Yet myths are many. In the past month, two people had been rescued from Colne mud banks, one man up to his neck. Just around the point on the Blackwater was where a wildfowler drowned. James Wentworth-Day wrote: "When they found him in the morning, he'd scraped a great hole in the mud big enough to hold a donkey cart. An' he was up to his shoulders in mud in the middle of it. Drowned! Pore chap!"

> With morbid glee, some say,
> Crabs take your eyes for their fresh watery content.

As the marsh water retreated, so giant footprints appeared. Someone had walked on wooden splatches. Ligger boards wrapped in chicken wire beckoned to mystery trade routes in the saltings. This was another smuggling country, many low-tide paths walked in the deep darks of moonless night. In the fifties, John Betjeman wrote of stackie barges:

> Far Essex fifty miles away,
> The level wastes of sucking mud,
> Where distant barges high with hay,
> Come sailing in upon the flood.

Trade has long moved from water to road. Yet our consumption addictions will play out here, as oceans warm and seas rise.

> With a shiver,
> The sandpipers went up with a whirr of wings and were smoke
> On the dome of the dusky air.
> The mud birds were on the move.

52. ANGELS IN THE BACK LANES

Showery rain spotted paving, then an Indian summer shone inside the whole valley. A term used in rural New York in the 1770s, thus derived from Native

Americans rather than the East Indies. On this continent, it was long a St. Luke's or St. Martin's summer, the latter for sun as late as November. Now there were memories of summer heat with the garden baked rich with color. Yet the light was lower, the shadows cooler, flowers in the hedges pale and gone over, thistledown thick by old man's beard smothering haw and hedge maple. The late sun turned the sky fiery orange, not at all like the hard blues of high June. This sumptuous light called for just sitting in the garden. A nearby mower was running, clunked, and silence. There were laughs, voices from other gardens, planes passing overhead. Goldfinch squabbled at the full feeders.

I looked afar, as once did Defoe and La Rochefoucauld, deciding to travel the valley one day, the county length the next. There were twenty-nine species in flower. On hedge bank were white trailing convolvulus, tall willowherb, sow thistle yellow and gone to explosions of seed floating on the air, many poppy and agrimony. On air were three perfumes for the seasons. Dusty harvest, straw on the roads, a musty heat in the air: the scent of summer. Autumn crackling of bonfire, fields swirling with gunmetal smoke. The sweet spring smell of cut grass. Winter is a desert, devoid of outdoor odor. Up at Workhouse Green, where was hardship and horror, a gaunt man sat on a bench beneath apple trees, by a patch of turned soil. His flat cap came up with country deliberation.

It had always been so: at first cold light, the land was quiet. But by seven labor was in the farmyards, tractor hitching polished plow, driver shaking shoulders, a day's work ahead trawling deep. The land would soon smell of damp soil. Gulls awaited, flickering white, ready to descend. Leaves were on most trees, though not horse chestnut. The national radio said, the coldest country place was Cavendish, at two degrees, in Suffolk. Misty souls twisted along river trails, and bottomless farm ponds billowed their cumulus. But even at that hour, drivers so hurried they would barely notice these particularities.

At Raydon airfield was hard standing where once rested airmen in canvas chairs, their wooden fighters lined beyond. Seventy generations of skylark have since scrambled. The road gutters were a gallery of cereal straw and bronzed onions. In one potato field gathered a hundred gulls, a mile away, a potato harvester was finishing. In the hedgerows were many blackberries.

The cloud cleared, the blue was streaked with contrails, sheared by high winds. A flick of right hand to other riders on the shadowed lanes. There was coffee and cake at sunny Snape, the café by the river mud, the barges bright and waders wheeping. In Westleton's village string on sheepwalks of hot sand, coming towards me was a cyclist in white sunglasses and familiar crouch. Then he was gone. It was the world's best sprinter riding the route for the Tour of Britain. It had become warm. A hedgehog scampered, leaping into a hedge.

In sunken lanes thirty feet deep with their own microclimate, amongst flick-ering shadow and spots of sunlight, were clouds of sparkling stars. Deepened by centuries of farm cart and horse, the light shone through leaf and tree, and insects had become angels dancing on air. The light came from within them.

A bleached tractor advanced. The spray booms were carelessly broad, the only escape up the grassy bank. The whiskery driver wallowed on metal seat. He scowled, stamped accelerator. People in queuing cars smiling their resignation too. Outsiders were always disrupters of rural rhythms.

Between flat fields was a man on a rusty bike behind two husky dogs rearing up and charging at the road. He smiled. More insects swarmed, safe now that swallows had departed. A straight road sheared through the purple heath, more than thirty pheasant bodies beaten down by vehicles on one short stretch.

Walberswick was past a ribbon of houses protected from summer invaders by yellow lines. My mother and I sat in the garden, still ablaze with color. We had glasses of white wine, and ate homemade pizza. Time slipped in the sunshine, cooled by onshore breeze. Inland to the railway station, the dust from dry plows and sandy roads filled the air, heat hissing from tarmac, high Suffolk at its best. In the sun at the station, two mothers planned an advance on London. The children bounced, the train came, we all went south.

I was eaten, bitten, burned, and older.
Though the hair has grayed,
There grows an inclination to walk by the great unknown.

———

53. SEASON OF MIST AND FIRE

It would be the hottest day ever for the month. But before crystal light burst through the mist, and blue appeared above, the dawn chorus was spring rich, the hilly toplands pillowed gray.

"Fog everywhere. Fog up the river . . . fog down the river . . . fog on the Essex marshes," began Charles Dickens in *Bleak House*.

On the Suffolk side of the valley you'd never know. Every field in fog, each meadow in mist. The land was enclosed. In the neighboring field was the muted sound of lost lambs and ewes. Sheep shapes appeared, began bleating. One spooked, they ran with thundering hooves, absorbed into silence. Under an ancient oak, the shrouded herd stood in fallen acorn and faded fescue.

The path skimming the hill is named for St. Edmund, one of many made by pilgrim feet to the town where the boy king was buried. Across the sunken lanes strung streamers of spiders' webs, their work broken in the damp. In hedges were gauzy orb and hanging bowers. On my arms, every hair was coated with opalescent droplets, my face and eyes too.

In one cloud,
A ghost horse stood hushed in silence.

Stands of bracken on sandy soil had been crushed into sleeping beds by deer, on fence posts single feathers pressed into split ends, so many warriors in the fog. Beneath a plucking post were drifts of pigeon down. Still the mist enclosed. At Poplar Farm, yellow leaves of fallen poplar were musty vinegar sweet and alluring. By a badgers' sett was a high hedge of holly wrapped with webs.

It was autumn, yet still in flower were mallow and harebell, yarrow and white campion, hawkweed and buttercup. High in hedge were bloody hip and haw, wild damson and blue-black sloe. The sun half-appeared at the end of the five-mile circuit, now those sheep glistened as the light flared from their woolly backs and heads.

One evening a yellow light appeared to the east, not flashing across the sky, just moving steadily from south to north. It was a burning bush, a piece of satellite, space architecture, slow and gold, yet gone before we could grab camera. Then a meteor surged across Siberian skies, videos recorded by drivers with looping cameras to protect against police violation. The shock waves shattered windows.

This was our life: in the afternoon, a fire in the incinerator flickered up garden brash. Every bird in the garden fell silent. Under the wide sky a keening buzzard circled slowly on summery thermals.

—◦◦◦◦◦—

54. IN MEMORIAM

In late afternoon, the sun can set and rise several times. Dropping down dark lanes, it falls into misty hills, on the tops it rises bloody red again. The air cooled rapidly, gardeners filling lanes with the smoke of heaped bonfire. There could be a hoary frost. Soon would be the time to gather sloe from hedgerow and plan for sweet gin on winter nights.

In days gone by, hedge and wood, roadside and meadow were natural food stores. Wild foods had always supplemented the raised: mushroom, blackberry, hedge apple and damson, rocket and sea purslane, white elderflower for champagne, red berries for wine. Also fish, wild birds, and eggs. With such collection came deep knowledge and understanding; it also brought conflict. Sitting magistrates were usually landowner squires, the strongest of penalties dealt to poachers. Wild foods are widely eaten across the world, on average eighty to a hundred species per location, in some countries up to a thousand. Diversity is good, and for many there is no great material difference between the farmed and the wild.

In our lands, a different predator is at work. There are now a million deer in England, eating much. Long gone the lynx and wolf and bear. Each year, up to fifty thousand traffic collisions involve a deer. The road has become a public abattoir.

Patrician pheasants never understood the motorcar,
In roadside grass feather explosions of dead pigeon,
Scattered and flung gray.
Squirrel and rabbit too, but never hare.
Roe and muntjac, stiff with rigor mortis,
Eroding over weeks to leather hide.
Badger rolled into green gutters,
Black and not white but stained tobacco yellow.
Hedgehog clipped and spun and flattened.
Never blackbird or thrush, weasel or fox.

Some seem to know, some not.

Once on a fast left bend a rook was hopping from foot to foot in agitation. In the road lay another bird. It pushed its partner with its beak, hopping back, and seemed so much to hope. Rooks mate for life.

On the way back a couple of hours later, there were two dead rooks in the road.

Two weeks ago, white feathers were strewn along the main road at the village south. One of the river swans lay with broken neck in false oat grass. In the village, car drivers slow for swan and ducks, for dim cats too, but on the trunk road, eyes are focused far away. Bashō wrote in 1694, not long before his death that year:

Along this road
This autumn eve
Is none but I.
　　Matsuo Bashō,
　　1644–1694

———◦———

55. THE RHYTHM OF FARM NAMES

On the kitchen table was a collection of many maps, connecting the route of a ride. There was poetry to the positions, each farm locked to its location and linked from south to north and then inland west. Timbered houses, stud and plaster, thatched or tiled, the small farms sold off as the bigger grew; on heathy sandlings dense with coconut gorse; near pine cathedrals dappled with sunlight; by humid potato fields irrigated by aerial booms; in valley and on windy top, places of crop and animal, bird and tree. Here was a tally, an enumeration of farm identities:

Valley Farm, in the vale
Rams Farm
Oak Farm

Lark Hall
Piper's West.

Acacia Farm, up by the war airfield and its skylarks
Corner Farm
Rookery Farm, with birds
Barrens Farm, without
Red House Farm, gone under new brick houses
Lux Farm and shop, meadows cut and the perfume of hay in the air.

Beaconhill Farm, near Playford's famed innovator of the agricultural
    revolution, Arthur Biddell
Creek Farm, by stinky sewage works
Decoy Farm, one of fourteen county decoys, sending five thousand ducks a
    year to city butchers.

Ufford Mill Farm
Park Farm, by another silent Decoy Farm at Ashe Abbey, the waters still
    and trim with lily pads
Quill Farm, at abandoned sandpits
Red House Farm, again, on the straight road to Blaxhall with its gray
    village hall
Stone Farm, where fellows who cut the hay believed the Blaxhall sandstone
    erratic grew from the ground, and gathered in the Ship Inn to sing and
    step dance.

Abbey Farm, at Snape Maltings
Rookery Farm, another, with free-range pigs and the rookery in pines over
    an ancient tumulus
Church Farm
Pattle's Farm
Redhouse Farm
Oak Tree Farm
Orchard Farm, and then Pretty Road through Theberton Woods of
    coppiced swidden and a pond of blue sky by the roadside.

Theberton Hill Farm, overlooking Minsmere wetlands and only a mile
    from the Eel's Foot singing pub at Eastbridge
Yewtree Farm, at Middleton, near Westleton: there is no Eastleton
Valley Farm and Hill Farm
Reckford Farm, at the stream that feeds the bird reserve, once remote
    enough for smuggler gangs.

Brick Kiln Farm, by buzzing heaths and sheepwalk country
Eastwood Lodge Farm, raising terriers and pheasants
Church Farm, by Reydon church, where was the funeral that wet summer
Hall Farm
Hillside Farm
Sotherton Low Farm, site of a deserted medieval village.

Lyons Farm, memories strong of the day we clambered into musty ruins,
    walls blue, roof blown, the farm family long gone
Walnut Tree Farm
Ivy Farm
Dairy Farm
Corner Farm. Again.

In those days, a single farm might have employed fifty men, down a shallow dip, thatched barn and stables, walled horse yard, threshing engine, a quarter-acre pond deep to swim a horse and soak tumbril wheels of ash, the plaster house painted Suffolk pink, patchy and stained and all an air of snugness. And jarred wrists from singling beet, rabbit and pigeon pests, rats in the roof and the tremble of dawn light as breath plumed and men stamped their hobnail boots.

Yet on these farms were dark tied cottages, dank and tiny, earth-filled walls, many to a bed. Only in the past century did rural children taste anything other than food boiled or raw. All craved sugar and fat, why birthday cakes were so special. Today they would find high street junk food quite miraculous. Yet their greatest trouble was often water: if there was no nearby spring or well, they might walk miles to fetch it in buckets. Drink all you can at school, children were told.

After harvest,
Joskins men bundled jerseys and oilskins,
Took a final swig of ale,
And walked to coast to join the herring boats.
They crossed to superstitions of water,
Now avoiding pigs and parsons.
The plowman stayed, the blacksmith too,
The forge the flaming draw for village gossip.

On farms are trapped spirits, those generations living long under the same names. Annie Dillard observed in "A Field of Silence," "the farm seemed eternal in the crude way the earth does—extending, that is, a very long time." We spiral down, may never come up.

OCTOBER

56. INSECT LIFE

Night frosts burnish autumn. Now days were filled with haze. Cumulus burst by fierce wind raced over blue sky, sheared trails crossing the upper air. Warmth brought flocks of greenfly, the village a bloom of busyness: paint seared from windowpane, churning concrete mixer, repointed brickwork. Leaves of poplar were on the road, the trees themselves bare. Always the last to turn, oak were tannin green.

The fields were part end of one season, part early next. A shift at the village surgery too, the roads chaotic and cars put up at all angles: winter flu jabs today. Along the valley road, scarred sugar beets in windrows were coated with loamy soil. Days ago, the same fields were glossy green and wet with irrigation prior to lifting, then worker tractors came to buzz by queen harvester until dusk descended. In the days of horse, a plowman walked eleven miles daily, could be plowing to February. It was a far period to fear rain: horsemen and plowmen sent home with no pay, wet washing meager shillings away. These days were dry, and now we soak the soil.

Cereal fields had already grown a green mist. Late one afternoon, gray-hooded jackdaw probed flinty soil, shadows dark and stretched towards far hedgerow. A lean roe deer picked across a harrowed field; it grew small and could have been a hare. Later, an antlered male stood stock-still in tall oat grass yellowed with evening glow. Straw leaked from a nearby barn, the yard had many midges. The swallows were long gone.

Now came migrant geese. Racing pigeons are bred for speed, but greylags are graceful. Driving around the county town, all the cars on the legal limit; an echelon slotted in to fly fifty feet above. We traveled for a mile or so, less than a lazy minute of steady wing beats, the geese shifting up-gear and pulling inland for evening roost.

To the garden came murmurs then shouts from a neighbor's. An archaeological expert had come, pits were being dug into the past across the village. Knowledge of ancient, medieval, and industrial history grew with finds of pottery and tile, rare arrowheads, recent pennies. Here had stood Trinovantes tribe, Roman soldier, sufferer of the Black Plague, shepherd, weaver who started the industrial revolution. Over here, there was water in the birdbaths, but one would not survive harsh winter's frost.

On the valley tops,
Out of gray-green oilseed delicate doves rose with the soothing rush of river,
No bustling wing-cracks of woodpigeon.
Turning back to the road;
There was a flash of orange and black.

And bang.

Horse-kicked by a hornet.
The chemical shock rippled around my mouth.
There were miles to go.
By home,
It was hard to breathe.

A truck from the timber yard delivered a half load, the tumbled logs lying out front. Inside, the woodstove waited.

―◦◦◦◦◦◦―

57. A NEW ANNIVERSARY

It was the dawning of a day. Gray light, racing dark clouds. Rain pooled on roof, fallen leaves in the garden glistened. Wind turned trees inside out. The whole atmosphere was on the move. The kettle boiled, and I pulled a chair and sat with tea at the open back door, bare feet tingling, robin then blackbird singing over the racing wind. There were four pink roses, two reds, two peach. Drips fell from the wisteria. The salmon hollyhock was crumpled silk, the sky reflected in flagstone sheen. I leant to see what would happen next. The feeders swung, empty. A rook dashed upwind. The hosepipe was laid out, the watering can also unnecessary for another season.

It was the dawn of another day. A new anniversary. I rose in silvered dark of moonlight, and drove towards Cassiopeia. The fields were wrapped with wisps of mist. A warmth smudged the east, a distant furnace beyond the underworld.

A bruised band of sky spread,
Trees and church towers emerging from darkness and cottony cover.
At Blythburgh, glassy water ebbed
From flooded marsh to river and raced

Towards the harbor.
A timeless light shone in the fogbank.

We drank tea, with resolve got going. This was not to be formal, where permissions are paid, as at institutional cemetery or graveyard. We went early to escape crowds. The sunrise was due a little after seven. My mother, brother, and I drove down to Blackshore, and with jackets zipped walked out on a wooden jetty. The pontoon bobbed on the outrushing river. All was composed. A redshank cried. Huge herring gulls perched on posts, but did not move.

The ashes were heavy, not at all like ash. The return was to the river that Dad painted so well, loved to watch, sailed on, swum in. We broadcast his ashes on the river, sowed them, scattered, tipped, let them run through our fingers. So many actions associated with broadcasting on the land, making ready to grow again. We took deep breaths, the moon fretted in the river at our feet. An old fisherman rolled along the track talking to his phone.

We left no sign. Many today are roadside memorials and named benches, the sacred wandering the land in the face of depersonalizing modernism. Many more are places hiding secrets. All we can do is face this rent in the fabric, close to the bones of nothingness and only words can be spoken. The grieving register, advised Seamus Heaney, is one that should never be completely shut off.

We let the river and its brown mud, its birds and the great cobalt dome, the boats and the anchor chains, let it all just seep up. A car pulled up towing a boat, the two men beginning to make ready. There was a haze of dawn blue in all the air. Out to sea the line of horizon-hugging clouds flared orange, the sun leaping up.

We hastened to the harbor-out, walking across marram dunes and sea pea mats. The ebbing river was smooth and as it met the choppy sea it curved north and east, a golden path to the heavens. On the harbor wall were more gulls, many smoky juveniles. Southwold itself floated above the mist on the marsh, a town in the cloud, the kind of mythical place you dream exists far above this flat world. It was still cold, five degrees. Downriver came the chugging fishing boat, and each man raised an arm slowly, nodding their heads upwards.

"All right," said one, smiling.

We turned inland for breakfast and hot coffee. The event, the scattering, was now much more. This day had been marked.

58. THINGS AND DOUBT

Rain lashed the land and wind tore through trees. It seemed best to look inward. It is good to pick up things when walking. Bird bones, stones with holes, seashells bleached and flints knapped, carved wood and bark beetle scarred, carnelian mineral and button badge, a brassy gun shell and golden amber containing the fossil memory of insects. Sometimes they come home. In my study are memory boxes, items tied to a particular place and time.

Not long ago, author Ian McEwan was coldly criticized for hurrying home with a handful of shingle. It was odd: it would take seventy thousand years to degrade Chesil Beach if each person in Britain took a kilogram every single week. He was creating a personal link through a thing, putting some story into material, in this case a handful of stones. Here it is: it came from a place.

An observation: Is part of our problem today something to do with the loss of story associated with the possessions we have? And so we throw them away, far too soon. More attachment may help to save this finite planet.

Here are three items.

Item 1: A fisherman friend, Eric Paisley, dredged up a dark bog oak from Benacre's underwater Neolithic forest, the archaic Doggerland. Two sides are cut smooth. It had been cared for, that oak post was held in the crusty hands of a craftsperson, then planted in a fence or house. It could be a few thousand years old or more. It is dense, not given to flighty possibilities. In the house, spiders never colonize. It stands on an east-facing windowsill.

Item 2: A self-winding watch my father obtained the day I was born. From a store tinder hot under corrugated iron roof, the desert stretching far. He handed it to me a few years ago. It snaps on wrist with springy precision. And stops if put down for a day. It tells only the time, no date or altitude, nor link to the Internet. It will go on working provided it is worn.

Item 3: A mobile phone. Very useful indeed. Made of rare metals, used many times daily, a platform for engagement with the wide world. But it is neither bog oak nor watch. It might last a couple of years more before the battery gives out. The screen is cracked, the camera lens foggy.

As my father lay in hospital back one June, I held a fragment of egg found on the Essex marsh, speckled gray-green and brown. He squinted, and said firmly, *lapwing*.

Then two days before he died,
Up flew the subject of skylarks,
Always singing over the warm cliffs by that bog oak's home.
I took the phone, clicked an app, and played a song of skylark.

"Lovely," said Dad.

"Such harmonious madness," wrote Shelley.

The bog oak and the phone. Both things of value. One proximal to a place, the other impervious to cultural difference and local expression.

How, then, could we guarantee the things we now own will last another thousand years or two? It could be our consumption culture is stimulated by a fading desire to tell stories. Pick stuff up, collect and store. Through their pasts, things might suggest a different future. This century is going to need a new club: to survive we must reduce the carbon intensity of our consumption by between ten- and one hundred–fold. At present, most economic growth causes damage to nature. There might be a stark choice: save the economy through growth; or save the finite planet.

Doubt is our product, once proudly boasted the tobacco industry. This poor planet cannot bear too much doubt. In the *Tao Te-Ching*, Lao-tzu wrote:

> Knowing what is enough is wealth . . .
> Hold your ground and you will last long.

—⟪⟫—

59. ALARM CALL

Another nightmare. It was a neighborhood of low lanes and dusty adobe. We were a group, armed but surrounded. We knew with visceral certainty we would die. It was the end. From the hill appeared my father tall and haloed in white. He beckoned, I followed back upslope, and woke soaked, but less iron-limbed than before, lying still and trying hard to breathe. Outside was the dripping of water from leaves, raindrops splashing on window, the curtains billowing inwards.

No need for alarm call: it was still the gloaming. A squall dashed from the east, wind gusting through the open kitchen door. A skein of cranky geese beat overhead. In the garden was scolding tic-tic-tic of wren, then chattering alarm call of dashing blackbird. Something was afoot. On the feeders were six balls of feather, family of long-tailed tits, spluttering in the tempest. Last week, there were eight.

Out in the valley, the air was damp and dense. There was wreckage from the rain. Branchlets of oak were down, conkers under horse chestnut smashed, tumbleweeds of leaves spinning along the road. Woodpigeon snapped wings, exploding out of trees to race over fields. They should be safe, the clouds too low for stooping peregrine, a mystery why so many individual pigeons dash alone at speed. The line of poplar by a fallen farmhouse was stripped bare, silent now till spring. Poplar rustle up a rushing river even on days when there is no wind. Now their yellow leaves rotted with rust. There was bright yellow maple, ash leaflets turned maroon, horse chestnut rusty but holding on. Beneath wild cherry were scarlet leaves veined with gold, the light from ground instead of sky.

In one field out on the tops, white overalls were tied to a stake with a white wizard hat. The scarecrow flapped and kicked, but could not escape. The field of young beet was white with gulls. Around the corner half a hundred rooks perched on telegraph wires, squawking, flapping wet wings. In the village of Bures, streets thronged with pealing bells, ringing out calls to prayer. Two people hobbled up the churchyard path. On the long road loped a leporid: *that poore hare*, seventy folk names and derogatory, the magic beast of dramatic speed and arching run of the dragon hillside itself.

This week, more controversies. A national tabloid routinely skeptical about science published what it called evidence that the planet had not warmed at all. An operation that lobbied for fossil fuel companies revealed it paid large sums to the party of government. Members of cabinet have taken against wind power, reduced subsidies for solar, slowed up nuclear. If the affluent cannot get it right, then why should the poorest? A scandal lingers on the local pages. The hospital had been manipulating waiting-list data to meet targets, putting it in the national dirty dozen.

Reason has not compelled us to care. Neither will a good future be a return to something rooted solely in the past. We need modern medical, farm and transport technology, our phones, robots, and many computers. Yet we need to break the current rules, bring the wilds to the city, create different aspirations. Greener economies in which material goods had not destroyed the planet would be good economies. There would be regular engagements with nature, whether in gardens or wild places, woods or fields, people doing things together that make these behaviors valued and worth repeating, people giving to others and making intergenerational links, communities investing time in activities that build contentment and well-being.

We have had alarm calls. Humankind cannot stand too much reality, cried T. S. Eliot's bird. As we sleep on watch, things worsen. There is, of course, a mathematical cruelty to the universe. We all die; the universe will end. But on the way, it could get grim.

Meanwhile, imagine a near future: black gold was finished. Its century and a half of miraculous cheap energy that was a touch to transport was over. It had blackened skies, expanded oceans, melted ice, made us complacent about energy. But then did come technologies turning to light, wave, wind, and plant for energy, packing and transferring it, which now all drove the environment-economy.

Being on the land offers an opportunity for small detachments from material goods and thoughts, and in return an intimacy with those things present. We already have everything; we just do not know it.

In the garden, a small black-and-copper beetle landed on my sleeve, climbed up my finger. It unfolded its elytra, flying into sunshine. The maples have turned fiery red. Two fields so recently harrowed were now a haze of green, wheat leaves rising fast in autumn warmth. Soon the clocks will change, the day darkening in the late afternoon.

60. THE SANDS OF ANOTHER SUMMER

Raid the inarticulate, recommended Seamus Heaney. Descend into the other. We are just on this journey. It was the warmest Halloween ever, twenty-three degrees, swirling starling above the roofs, racing under the darkling sky. It used to be this way. It never was this way. Late flowering or early: double summer for the pale blue ceanothus, in flower again; one spring scarlet azalea. Purple delphinium have come again. Still rudbeckia flowers and yet leaves fall from the maples.

There were distant ticks of two clocks. A female deer was at the bottom of the garden. A fawn flashed white tail and bounced on the grass. The mother nudged it onwards. Perhaps it had just been born. Bees followed sun to flower, a grasshopper bathing on the wood-wasp-scoured bench. Bright mosquitoes danced, a ladybird fell and bounced from a page. Rooks cawed, gulls cried white on the blue sky.

There were flutters of rain, then gone again. At Wakering Stairs, people milled by wind-washed seawall, and looked at the most dangerous road in Britain. The water was out by the wind turbines and solid ships elevated above the sandbanks and swatchways. Surely not, not that long ago. But it was years. The last Broomway walk, then in scorching summer, now an autumn pretending to be summer. Everyone had grown older. Brian and Toni Dawson fetched photos of their grown daughter at college, with their horse on Lundy. Time had slipped into mud, drowned each tide one upon the next.

The light was here and above and below. Wet sands, blue rills, streaked trails. A blustery wind rose. It was a walk for wellingtons, yet bare feet would have been fine, even for viscous mud at Asplins Head. Walkers splashed, mud sucked. Beyond the seawall were ammunition dumps and shells of faded red. Foulness Island was silent, no cricket or grasshopper, no bare-knuckle fighter as in the old days. Lime-green pebbles were in the salt water, stained with chlorophyll from the sea grass.

There were miles of the Maplins stretching to the setting sun, bright and glittering on the wet sand and under the silver sky. Dark figures cast shadows on mud and sand, on shell and ragworm and tidal ripple pocked by feet of brent geese and herring gull. Far away was the land of people. Out here was the world of fish and bird, people inarticulate in the face of low sun, their voices scattered far by wind.

Let me do it.
Let me walk on the thin layer
Of water,
Where the sea so stealthily covers flats to the coast.
The sun fell fast.
The tide dashed inwards, the sands were gone.
The sea and breeze, the heat and geese.
Wind-torn memories all saved in salt.

61. WAIT FOR THE END

A great storm loomed. Trains were canceled. Much rain and dangerous wind were forecast. But overreaction was also predicted. It was just autumn weather, a little extreme, nothing more.

On the circular walk from Arger Fen to Bures, the sun blazed from the round moraine hills and lines of young wheat shivered in the wind. Auras formed around Ronaldsay sheep, skittering across the meadow. Twenty plants were still in flower, ink cap mushrooms tall in grass. It was warm for the time of year, or at least how it used to be, soggy underfoot. Many acorns were on the ground, a mast year. Would oak survive the night gale, great sails of leaves but anchored tight? On the path was a dead pigeon, half-consumed, feathers strewn in stems of grass. Bubbling stream, no otter. No buzzards either. Pigeon raced downwind while jackdaw yapped and played. In the meadow turf of the far hillside was carved the white dragon, the serpent staring back as does the medieval worm on the valley church wall.

My son called to say he saved a life. On a south London street, an old man collapsed on the pavement. He stepped in amidst the crowd and pumped his chest until the ambulance drew up. The local hospital here had meantime descended into more mayhem. There is no way back once you have been on the front pages. No one was surprised. My daughter had to book the doctor on a private track, the public queues unmanaged, and he nodded and said her back brace could come off. She would be climbing again soon.

Darkness came early, the clocks had changed. The lawn was covered with hawthorn leaf. Yet lavender rubbed between palms still smelled of summer heat. Soon it will be the month when people blink, outside the mole catcher at work and inside office people making decisions at a time when they bend under stress. Daylight will be scant, the time since last holiday lengthening. Yet Christmas is far away too. Never decide anything serious in November, when the garden is going over and darkness draws in fast.

A wren scolds, goldfinch glitter, winds scowl.

NOVEMBER

62. BONFIRE NIGHT

It was the time of feast and fire. Wind had lashed the last leaf from ash and maple, and wood pigeon had found their autumn flocks. In the field, cold men in camouflage waved flags and stumbled towards woods where hid the guns. If pheasants had evolved an alarm run, they might escape. But they have not. The land echoed to crack and thump. A flock of rooks sang safe stories in a bare poplar. Still in hedgerow were fennel and hogweed, blackberries gone to dust. Old folklore says red hips and haws promise winters cold and long. This day, rain fell heavily. There could be disappointment, yet at evening all was dry. Families converged on the village playing field.

Smoke billowed from barbecue, steam from pans of mulled wine. Children waved sparklers and skipped, neon bands fused to necks and wrists. Villagers shared the latest news. Only a week after the clocks had changed, seven before Christmas, all had gathered to remember a failure to bomb Parliament. But long lingers confusion: Is Guy Fawkes Day about attempt or foiling?

The bonfire crackled, wood smoke swirling up towards the cloud. Up went the fireworks, primary bang, secondary swish, fancy pop, and stars cast across the heavens. Rockets arched high, children cried *woo*, others clapping hands over ears and running to the village hall to peer from behind glass. How glittering lights grip the imagination, cities at night offering safe destination and hope. Many are the ways to claim local territory: beating the bounds, mud race, cheese rolling, pilgrimage, farmers' market, horse fair, vegetable competition. By being builders of common culture, participants and spectators assert identity. Some are rare: carnival, street party; some long gone: people of the east no longer strap up heavy skates to glide on frozen fen and icy dike.

The end was sudden and sad. There was a ripple of applause, the burgers and hot dogs now half price. Someone threw a firework on the fire, the rocket shooting sideways at nearby houses. There was dark muttering. Figures ambled to the bonfire, their faces savage in the flickering flame. Gradually groups dispersed to warm houses and delayed homework, the playing field quiet again.

"Ashes do not come to firewood," wrote Dōgen Zenji.

Next year will be another mound of wood and waste to burn, the people gathering again.

⟞⟨⟩⟞

63. AT FIRST, SILENCE

The valley was capped by cloud. Essex had been cut off, over river. Leaves covered lawns, evidence of hard winds. The trees were still. Oak had begun to turn, tingeing russet, others dipped in gold. At the top of Clicket Hill two were resolute, each year the valley's last to succumb. This winter they could be green come January. In hedges tumbled with old man's beard, songbirds were quiet; in skies nothing flew through the heavy air.

A marble egret rose on wide wings,
And drifted slowly down.
In a shady orchard, sheep lay sleeping.

The day started gray, dimmed, and got dark. On two days, two minutes' human silence were observed for the fallen. Long before, St. Martin's Eve was for a rural reckoning, animals slaughtered and salted, the final fresh meat until spring. Tales were told at feasts to fend off darkening nights; many thought of St. Martin as patron of the drunkard.

Yet slowly the valley seemed to waken. Sounds emerged. A flock of rooks was in the wheat stubble, rising as flakes of chattering charcoal. At the four corners by sugar beet windrows, two of John Rix's men were standing at the harvester, its working life stilled. Above was the liquid song of skylark, streaming memories of spring. Hoy, we saluted, they shouted back. On the misty top by the TV masts, top lamps blinking red, high-voltage lines leaked electrons in a telegraphic buzz. Where previously had been strutting pheasants was only silence. Twenty million reared and released each year. A horse thudded across a paddock, stamping to a halt. It turned away. A tall woman walked a sleek black dog. On an open stretch, a sparrowhawk circled, swooping up to a bare ash.

Standing later in the garden; autumn insects came too: bumblebee in hollyhock, wood wasp by the fence, a swarm of ladybird awake from hibernation. Hyacinth were sprouting, buds might burst of azalea. Mrs. Paine's geraniums were richly scarlet, Cedric Morris's pale pink also in flower. All the roses were on last blooms. In five weeks would be the short day of solstice. The shock of silent winter was still to strike.

—————

64. THE NIGHT HOURS

Night hours seemed endless; before dawn a thrush sang sanity from a treetop. A blush of pink lined the eastern sky, far above thin streaks of altostratus hinted of the storm out west. Cold gripped, wind ripped, the last leaves gone from silver birch. From the east, rooks sailed across the wind, angled at their destination. From the west, a flock of two hundred jackdaw tumbled in the sky. Caw and kraa and antiphonal chack. At outer space, airliners furrowed deep, trailing gas lines in thin air. A dark heron filled the sky, a whistle of feathers, still the thrush singing on. If I were retired, I could just sit here until afternoon, then doze off for a long nap.

Light filled the gauzy garden. Leaves had filled the beds. Scarlet geraniums still climbed by white rose; purple scabious by a red. These remains of warm days had now met bolting daffodils, a foot high already. The delphinium were confused, sprouting feed for snails. In the valley, yellow mustard filled fields with pepper. Now blue tit seeped and swooped to the feeders. A flock of fifty wood pigeon passed, one diving down with folded wings. Two doves perched on the eucalyptus, wheezing. In the Faroe sheep isles, winter winds of 130 miles per hour; over here, it was winter-autumn-spring at once. What hope was there for the climate conference in South Africa? None of us wish to go gentle into that night: it won't be good.

On the way to the hospital I stopped at the seaside, parking by a house that was our house, bedrooms looking at the churning bay. The moon was a waxing crescent, the tide dangerously high. A century ago, Thomas Hardy stayed in Southwold, writing in a letter, "Cloudless weather here, and splendid air." Waves advanced from the southeast, rumbled up, rushing over groynes, thumping onto the beach, tugging at the promenade. A spray filled all the air.

Yet from this drama, the sun shone from inside the storm's high clouds, the sea becoming molten mercury.

> Good men, the last wave by, crying how bright
> Their frail deeds might have danced in a green bay.

For Dylan Thomas, for us all, this is it: all will rage against the dying of the light.

—————

65. LEAF FALL AND MISTS

Normal November. A slow-moving front halted. Mizzle filled the air, wind tugged at bush and branch. Up and down the valley, the colors associated with pre-Halloween were rich long after ritual of firework and the village choir's singing of Fauré's Requiem in the stone-cold church.

The light was from the land. Beneath maple and sycamore were mirror trees plastered on wet road. Yellow, gold, russet, orange, trees glued to tarmac. In deep lanes, wind blew rivers of leaf, spinning slow dancers, gathered in gutters, piled in lines that linked one field to another. In the stubble of zero-tilled fields where wheat will sprout, a rook row probed a tramline. Leaves swirled, soon to rot and decay, mildew and rust to come, skeleton ribs and then back to soil.

A new invader stalks. It stole in two years ago, or was it three, and no one noticed. Now despair. Ash die back. Chalara fungal spores came on winds across the sea, also on young trees purchased from afar. So, some questions. Why was such stock so cheap, why so easy to obtain? Now a threat to 90 million trees. Ash was never just a tree: it was plow, harrow, spade, and axe. It was the fellows of cart wheels, the wheelwright choosing tough roadside trees rather than those from soft meadows. The tree disease invasions just keep coming, the leaves keep falling.

Beneath the gray sky, longhorn cattle grazed green meadows, white sheep standing mixed with inky corvids. On a maple perched a sentinel rook, cawing warning. Mid-November, many flowers in the hedges. Purple mallow and dead nettle, lemony thistle, much yarrow cream and pink. Bolted rape volunteers lined one field side. Clumps of white hogweed, the book of old authority says "fl. 6–7." Many flowers are beyond their historic zones of comfort. Still, many farmers say every year has extremes.

On one sandy bank of acid grass was a blood-red poppy, now in the same month as the paper poppy pinned to breast. Above land and beneath sky circled square-tailed buzzards, watching wet meadow by the river.

One day came up bright and brilliant. Frost was thick on the roof, fogbanks following the river. Low sun lanced through woodland, warming clay sod, raising up wraiths of mist. A house gushed steam from a condensing boiler, filling up the road.

On field tops, after sun had crawled above the trees,
A red tractor breezed forth and back over rape with booms outspread.
No peace for farmworkers:
Sunday morning sunshine and a day for work.
The spray was on the field, in the lane, in the lungs.
It was hard to breathe.

Still the sun shone, the garden maples blazed. Rook and gull were black and white. The small family of long-tailed tits bubbled around the seed and nuts. One exploded in the sunlight refracted through its feathers, a ball not of bird but whirring light, flew towards me, swerving at the last and into a tree. Each followed, the sun in feather and wing beat, these birds missing by an inch.

One Sunday I drove to Leigh-on-Sea to speak at Rachel Lichtenstein and Colette Bailey's Shorelines festival. The sky was still clear, the sunlight brilliant. Above the southeast horizon was a single white cloud. The café in the community center was bustling, coffee warm, toast crisp. There was song, photo, film, and talks of wild and industrial, typically side by side on this coast. There were old friends, books to sign.

In came cold, now we hunched before the stove, the fire bright and glowing. Resin filled the room.

An eternal hope: "Sempiternum requiem," sang the choir in the church.

66. BEACH FISHERMEN AND WATER SPRITES

On the cliff-top greensward was a tribe of gulls. The bungalows had sea views, yet rills of guano streaked the tiles. The gray clouds were low, the vacant harbor lost in fog, wind turbines gone too. On this raw day, two groups were out, beach seadog and dog walker. One relaxed and observant, the other determined, keen to get back.

The hospital car park was mostly empty. Welcome to the madhouse, chirped one of the ladies on the ward, all laughing. We awaited news from the operators. The anesthetist followed a checklist of questions, but his flies were undone. The surgeon tipped his head, asking what my mother was in for, and with a felt pen drew an arrow on her knee. Welcome indeed.

At the beach, fishermen faced waves foaming on shingly stone, looking with hope. Meanwhile, across the Atlantic Superstorm Sandy thrashed the eastern seaboard. Some get the message; many do not. We could name hurricane and tropical storm after oil companies. In Sebald's book of fables, *The Rings of Saturn*, he watched fishermen camped on the beach, a few miles to the south, and wrote, "They just want to be in a place where they have the world behind them, and before them nothing but emptiness." Fishermen do not see the sea as empty, but they do want the world to go away.

"What are you hoping for?"

A thin man wearing felt hat and flaps opened his calloused hands a little, then outstretched, smiling. "Oh, a cod about this long!"

The two old boys laughed. A cod or whiting, a bass if they were running, a tasty dab. They were down from inland Norfolk, just for the day, faces etched by life outdoors. They talked too of great gray predators, mermaid seals swimming south from Horsey rookery, hiding in waves, nipping in and lifting fish from the hook.

Adults can weigh three hundred kilograms; there is no gain in arguing, a hint of pride in their behavior.

The idea of a lovable mermaid is a recent invention, and oddly wrong. Inland, the freshwater mermaid was the bugbear, a water sprite of river and deep pond snaring passers-by. Children especially, and they knew it. "Them nasty things what hook you into the water," states one boy in Jennifer Westwood and Jacqueline Simpson's *Lore of the Land*. Not long ago, there was widespread fear of drowning, rivers ominous, wells for wishing but ponds for slipping, the sea itself where men and boys walked the seabed. Mermaids drowned sailors, all the time. Up near the seals is Haisboro' Sands and a deadly reach called the Devil's Throat, HMS *Invincible* going down in a storm with the loss of four hundred. Soon will be the anniversary of the North Sea's disastrous Great Tide: three hundred drowned along this shore. As in the Americas, water sprites will not be short of future business.

The waves lapped quietly, then shimmering silver dashed across the water. The clouds split, but the blue was gone again. To the south, sandstone cliffs were crumbling and signs on the tops said: *Keep Out, Golf Course*. Below were clumps of tree lupin, thin palmate leaves, tough-stemmed, stabilizing the drifty dunes. Romans introduced food lupin to Britain, but these came from California in the 1790s. A couple of pale yellow flowers remained, there was a handful of seeds to be gathered for the garden. On cliff, wren and robin squabbled, chaffinch dashed from bush to bush. Just south was the hamlet of Newton, once on maps and now on seabed.

Beyond the tussocks of sharp marram, one fisherman held a whiting, and grabbed up four rigs lost by others. It was a tangle of green nylon and lead weights, patience needed for winding out the lines, saving the lead. At the beach café, metal tables shone on the promenade. A shag beat across wind under inky cloud. The turbines popped into view, and watery sun fell upon the old fishing town. The catch of centuries was king herring, since at least the Domesday Book, yet today there were no boats. It was a slow walk up cliff and back to the hospital.

That evening, a huge full moon rose over the east of the garden. It seemed pinned to the sky. On the cold grass, shadows of orchard trees stretched in silver light.

—⟨⟩—

67. MUCH CAN CHANGE IN A SHORT TIME

The ploughed fields were stilled seas, brown waves crumpled.
Many a road was lost under water,
Pouring from fields,
Gushing from field drain, rushing down slope.
More rain fell.

There were a hundred flood alerts, a hundred warnings, then overspill and breach. Insurance companies forecast withdrawal from lowlands in favor of profit. The elderly were pulled from cars and upper-story windows, ferried by rescue boats. Canoes paddled along streets, lifeboats sculled over meadows. Leisure centers were filled with emergency beds and care provisions. This was not Katrina, but what was worse: the probable consequences of climate change, or the earnest politicians? In the west, valleys had become shimmering lakes of sky, houses rimed with mud, cattle stranded on pasture islands. In our valley, the Stour was in the water meadows. Then deep lows darted fast for the Mediterranean, northerlies howling in. It would become clear and frosty, winter walking the land.

All Souls' Day was November's second, a time to linger on the ghost, consider charity for the living. The end of the month was marked by days of saints: St. Hugh's, St. Cecilia's, St. Clement's, St. Catherine's, St. Andrew's. Each was a custom of feast and visit for sweet and soul cake eaten for rhymes recited or songs sung. There is something to say for a revival of clementing and catterning, even souling for walking and talking. But rural late November was also for the hiring fair: rehired good, but left standing and winter loomed long and bitter, the workhouse enforced for many.

Three days ago we walked uphill and over the back. The sun was shining, the sky hard and land sodden. The colors of leaves were underfoot. Field portions were still maize and sorghum cover for game. In the distance guns cracked and pheasants fell. We walked paths that crossed stony fields from corner to corner. There was a rash of molehills. Some green wheat was high, other fields patchy. A horseman thudded by on a gray, splashing mud from sunken lane. Drier back there, he waved, staring ahead. Hidden golfers boasted of smashing balls far, but there were plinks and cries of disappointment. Badger had deposited drifts of sand down walls of the green lane. High above, the leaves of oak were burnished bronze on the clear sky.

Dusk brought anxious cries of tawny owl. The moon was almost full, flying silver bright above racing clouds, the wind sharp. The lawn needed raking, one compost bin was filled with piles of copper beech and birch, lilac and hawthorn, wild cherry. Now all in rotting darkness. Next day: the lawn was covered again. Stanley Kunitz wrote that every garden is an imaginative construct, a wild braid. In one corner perhaps something new, maybe maples and a Japanese theme. As the log fire crackled, the pots protected, so plans could be hatched for spring. It was a winter luxury: brief excursions, longer by the fire, time to dream ahead.

Christmas lights were up, creeping ever more into autumn. Today's economy deals loss and pain. Jobs lost, some gained. It was the modern hiring fair. Someone will say: the way to save the economy would be to spend more. But the moon stares down on one planet, and we are consuming it to death. Yet the things we fear might lose their power. Then drama from the magistrates: the developer on the far side of the valley was declared bankrupt. Local celebration, but wait: order would be restored. The land was to be sold and pennies in the pound repaid. A year later the new owner smiled and published plans for swathes of shops and houses. The valley awaits a different scar, another narrative about being the good guys.

The dark garden was cold and silver, the skeletal trees dark against the top-lit clouds, shadows spread by the moon. Another tawny's cry widened the spaces inside the night. In this way November elided to December. Customs and nature have defined social stability. Both are being eroded. Much can change, in a short time.

---

68. PASSING YEARS

The train stumbled through towers and tracks and wastelands, swinging to face the city in the sky. Christmas lights were bright between banks and offices lit by the glow of financial scandal. The doors hissed open, clunked closed, passengers on board, Canary Wharf passed to land beyond the river. A boy hung from the ceiling, hooting. Others were blank. Several talked to phones, some mumbling, others at volume. Through narrowed eyes, it was time to rehearse.

Greenwich was a glittering market, but the maritime museum was lost. Backtracking; the main entrance was where it should be. "Lost at Sea" was an evening of song and art. There were rum tots, inside glows, soaring sea-songs from fishermen's wives. The audience was attentive, laughed and smiled, bought books. An old colleague came, with friends, last met twenty years before. The light railway clattered north, linking with a junk-food shuttle, the carriage full of sweat and grease and faces tired from the late hire.

The Dog Star was in the west, the sky meshed with rippled cloud. It was quiet, save for cars on the hill. A beast crashed in bushes at the garden end and silence fell. There was no other natural sound. It was the time to move a hundred pots up to the house. The many maples huddled, a hollow rent where once weaved delicate froths of fiery red. All was still. In the far distance was a sodium streetlight.

It was the last day of November.
Everything else was pared back,
Hunkered down,
Awaiting winter's ascension.
The garden tawny cried.
The years keep passing, flowing faster.
Breathe deeply, think little.
Look at the light, feel fresh wind.
Taste the food,
Lay head on pillow and hope to dream.

DECEMBER

69. A MARSH MURMURATION

Welcome to the whisperers. Inside the Suffolk coast, soothing reeds flank stream and creeks pool at brackish broads. The inner Blyth banks broke in fifty-three, much later meadows flooded and Wolsey Creek diverted through the shivering shires of Hen Reedbeds. Here trot tan Tarpan horse to open up the reed, and in spring will be clover and trefoil rich with bees. In summer, at perch posts in the water will squabble ticking terns, recovered otter and water vole back all year. The lucky now hear the boom of bittern, once a fenman's favored Sunday roast, everywhere now icon for the rare.

It was murky winter at the reed beds, half light before dusk. Small flocks of starlings from far had started flighting low, fast and knowing. In the crisp teeth of a northerly, they were meeting for a murmuration. It has become normal for common birds to be less valued than the rare. Yet here was a starry spectacle.

These great mimics,
Wheezers,
Medieval pets, were soundless
As thirty thousand pairs of wings beat on atomic air.
They flowed across the sky,
The flock swelling as arrivals seamed with shape-shifting smoke.
They turned together,
Disappearing in the western eye.
With a flick the cloak was dark and pressed.
Some rushed rank and pulled elastic,
Failing and rippling back to join the liquid mass.
Hawks might work havoc,
But the flock flashed unworried,
Back above the muds.

A winter wildfowler from north Essex, Peter Avery, looked at coastal marsh and wrote: "The mud is grey, the sky grey, the saltmarsh brown. The place is wild, at its best. Packs of wigeon come in high, teal asleep at the water's edge, waders feeding ahead of the flooding tide. The thrill of being out with wild birds never lessens."

Here cloud to the sea and lighthouse on the town tops turned pink, to the west the sun had sunk but the sky was alight beyond dark cumulus. The murmuration swept far inland, then up high, a ferment across the road to the town, to reeds by the salty lido.

As dark fell, the birds voted.
The pilgrims formed
A tall tornado.
Within seconds,
They were sucked into the reeds,
Yet bubbled up,
Leapfrogging inwards.
All were inside.

At thirty grams a bird, densities of five hundred in each cubic meter, those reeds will be flattened. The cold sky yawned.

Night was complete. We walked back to welcome warmth.

⟆⟏⟍⟋⟏⟎

70. POOR MAN'S HEAVEN

The solstice approached. Soon days would lengthen, though only by a minute daily until the new year. Clear nights brought hard frost, dimmed daylight hours of rushing fronts, drizzle one day, wet snow another. The crescent moon waned, rising at one in the morning and setting at noon. The sun would be down at a quarter to four. The long night of winter draws tribes together.

In the garden, dawn washed trees and brickwork. Samuel Bensusan wrote, "You can learn a lot in the country by sitting doing nothing." Birds came: blackbird rich and mellow, squabbling robin, fighting on a feeder. No groups for them. Overhead rook and jackdaw had congregated into great flocks, later striding across the back pasture, probing the cold soil. Then came gregarious gulls, cleaving distance with a twitch of angled wings. There was much to learn on gull variability: winter or summer plumage, juvenile or adult, black-tipped wings, dark ear patches, colored legs. Outside pigeon packs raced in stable formation over poplar. Later spangled starling destroyed fat balls at the feeders. They fought one another, squeaking and leaping, ignoring tiny goldfinch and tit, dashing from junior angles.

Frost was hard and burned lungs. Puddles were solid with ice, crushed where cars had passed. On tight corners, the bike twitched on the rimed road. Other tribes were abroad. Dogs and their walkers, some striding out with Labradors, black and sleek; others elderly and slow with grayed whiskers. In the village at the far valley end, church bells called those in furs. It was a bracing morning. Up at Workhouse Green, a couple stopped, holding close their dog with hind legs strapped to wheels. The Clickett Hill oaks were still golden green; all other woodlands skeletal. By the river, brown bundles of Ronaldsay sheep bleated from an iced meadow.

"Bit nippy," declared a bowed woman with red head scarf, walking her whiskered greyhounds. We smiled. It seemed to be dark from midday. There was nothing to fear.

For this was once the time for great gatherings in the Suffolk singing pubs. The men were farmworker and laborer, railwayman and horseman, gardener and gamekeeper; some went fishing on herring boats. The women worked the big houses and dairies. All crammed in snugs and wooden pews at the Eel's Foot, the Ship Inn, the Green Man: all were singers and step dancers. In the flickering light of oil lamp, beer drawn from barrel and a haze of tobacco smoke, *Good order, please*, called the chairman, and someone would stand, hat in hand, and sing "The Blackbird," "The Barley Mow," "The Dark-Eyed Sailor." A mumble of voices, a laugh, then silenced and all joining the song chorus. Louisa Howard was renowned step dancer, up on table and bent double under the low ceiling. Lightning Jack the old sailor made sparks fly, dancing in boots big with hobnails. Tom Goddard, both poacher and gamekeeper, sang an anthem of hope for their tribe, "Poor Man's Heaven," and in the crowd was counterpoint commentary.

> . . . in poor man's heaven
> We'll own our own home   [that'd be nice]
> And we won't have to work like a slave   [that's what we want]
> But we will be proud, to sing right out loud   [all joining in now]
> The land of the free and the brave.
> And good luck, good luck, to the barley mow.

Surprise: then came snow. Eight hours of tinkling flakes, accumulating well. Some winters pass now with no snowfall. In the garden, all was silent. It was long since dark, yet it seemed as if snow and low sky were manufacturing light. It is never dark with snow. The satellite signal failed. The ladder was heavy, the dish cleared with gloveless hands. Call from inside. It was working. Later we put up the tree, and ate mince pies with mulled wine.

The next morning, the snow was all patinated petroglyphs where bird feet stamped. Later came the glory of goldfinch, a scrambling charm of forty on the feeders.

71. DARK AND WET AT THE SOLSTICE

It had always been so: hours of gloaming and little possibility. Dusk, night, dawn, just; then dusk. It felt it was the end of things and times. Some days fog filled the valley, wrapping all the land.

> All was quiet inside a gray blanket.
> Warm air, more moisture,
> Drops more too,
> It had been the wettest month on record.
> It rained for twenty-four hours unbroken.
> Across the country,
> Christmas season was welcomed by hundreds more flood warnings.
> Kierkegaard wrote, too much possibility leads to the madhouse.

In the press, there were bonuses for bankers, coincidental price rises announced by each big energy company. Simpler lives may be an answer, in which we are here to be here. The valley was underwater, good floods on meadow rather than in house. March had hosepipe ban; now every rod of land was sodden, water running fast off every gradient. The vale filled with wetland birds, gliding in to splash the glassy land.

Tile drains gushed from fields, each ditch and dike full and overflowed. Clay sod in fields glistened, slumped with the weight of wet. One hillside lane was a rushing river of soily water. There was dripping, trickling, rushing, dribbling. So much water on the tops and in small tributaries that the main valley floor could be flooded forever. In sunken lanes, individual cow parsley had grown a foot high, bright and green. There was one dandelion yellow in banks of rotted leaves. The subsiding economy had delivered danger: many back roads now abandoned. Cracks and potholes have opened wide, a surface puddle can hide a jagged deep. Broken hubcaps are propped at hedge banks.

The skin needs sunlight, or we would have too little vitamin D. Yet there was no sun. Lack results in children's rickets, exacerbates osteoporosis and osteomalacia in adults, raises risk for cancers, multiple sclerosis, cardiovascular disease, and rheumatoid arthritis. It is a long list. Inside, of course, are the blinking lights of Christmas trees, glowing log fires. The allure of artificial light seems greatest at the time of the shortest day.

One gray day, old fence posts received repair. The northern garden edge had been untouched these twenty years. Geese were heard, not seen, then flew low, heading east. A tamarisk and holly got the chop. A great pile of vegetation rose on the lawn. There was dragging, pulling, carrying. Inside waited warming tea.

There was a school prize giving at Thomas Mills, up at the county center. Teachers and governors took glasses of sherry, left library for the hall. There were smiling students, books and cups, shaken hands and parent pride. An extra moment for the daughter of two of my publishers, Alice, on the way to greater things. Then a short speech on consumption and possessions, our creaking planet, from the bag came bog oak, watch, and phone. Look at this, and this. And what about your challenge as artists and musicians, scientists and storytellers, lawyers and linguists? You each have a part to play in making your future livable and happy, for we are failing. On the way home, there was gray snow piled in hedges, then came fast a front of rain and as wet met cold, sleet drove dense from looming dark.

Yet the night was lovely. A little owl hopped in the road, a tawny flashed from tree to tree, a barn owl ghostly flapped the night. A russet fox jumped and stitched into a hedge. A muntjac stood stiffly in long grass.

Wind had gathered leaves in piles at the garden edge. All was quiet, the car engine ticking in the dark.

72. PRUNING AND PLANNING

Rain sluiced from inky clouds, and the trunks of two apple trees turned bronze. Water dripped on glossed bamboo. The mossy lawn was soft and spongy. For years the apple and pear had passed undisturbed. But now a pruning, a rightful return to proper shape. They were snipped and cut and chopped and sawed. A large bird cherry had sprung up, sixteen inches round. It was a weight to drag. The inside canopies were clipped, spurs cleared, new shapes emerging. The rain stopped, the western sky growing pale then bright, and twig and branch were silhouettes. The garden tawny cried, all the other birds still for night.

The stepladder sat in piles of brash; there was more work to come. There would be chopping before logs emerged. Once upon a time, there would have been water to draw. Resting in the pale sun, a throstle hopped on my foot.

It was no longer the end of autumn promising long winter; it felt falsely of spring. There would be snow and frost, yet days were lengthening. There were mite galls to snip from golden broom, the infection spread so fast since summer. A butcher's broom fell beneath the clipper, a sprawling bush now neat. Above rooks beat upwind, then down, falling playfully, continued on home. Two blackbirds pattered feet, tipping heads always left. They swiftly stabbed with yellow beak, a worm emerging every time.

The lower garden could be ready for some new style. There might be raked gravel, an island of rocks, moss on stones. Four dissected maples awaited planting. It was good to plan. Such is the nature of gardens, such too the gardening of nature. Inside the bright tree filled the house with scented spruce.

The night was dreamless,
The sun climbed into airless cold sky,
We pruned some more.
Branches now awaiting the shredder.

—⊶⊷—

73. DARK AND WET, AGAIN

Gray morning, cold. Above, the cover thin, then gone. The sun climbed in the hilltop trees, all morning never more than a hand span high. The sky was polarized blue, roads turning silver as they wound in deep lanes. It was window weather, colder than it looked, the westerlies harsh, the sun weak. Pairs of rook gleamed glossy in the kale and wheat, searching frozen seas of clay. There were windrows of crisped leaves in the gutter, and sheared trees, cast down by last week's storm, the tide surging up the North Sea to finish higher than in fifty-three. Many floods, but no catastrophe. These days there is data minute by minute, detailed maps and digital modeling. Sixty years ago, the wind roared but no one knew a thing, until the cold sea crashed in.

A stop again at Hen Reedbeds, the car park this time empty. The air was cold and clear, the east wind biting. A huge sky leaked heat to heaven. There were warnings on a long barrow. The river wall had collapsed, the surge crept inside and attacked from the wrong side. Soil and clay and grass had slumped, but the wall had held.

A barn owl flighted up from reeds and quartered back and forth. Another ghosted by a creek, flying by marsh and mud and field. It perched on a post out on the estuary. The town was in the east across the slapping gray-blue water. The tide was low, mud oozing, the sky down here and up there too. It was cold as the bones in the barrow.

Then a flashing flock appeared, racing over Tinker's Marshes. The murmuration swerved, contracted and expanded as it breathed. They seemed to be further out than before, but were a group of only thirty birds, flashing above the rustling reed. No more came. On this side once was Bulcamp Workhouse, the worst in the known world, malnourished men and women abandoned to a life on hard chairs, a huge bare room, empty and hopeless. The interwar district nurse was appalled: "You'd never think they'd spent all those years in the beautiful fields."

There were a thousand gulls,
Breezed from wasteland tip to marsh safe for night.
Out on mudflat were trees reflected from the shore.
Rain dashed down.
On the Blyth,

Duck gabbled, curlew warbled.
Below the western sky, a blush was on the muddy moisture,
The water tower alone and tall.
All else was flat and low,
The brain just winding to a halt.

All else had gone and the world was filled by birds and warning cries of redshank, the seawall soft and tide arising. To stop would be to freeze forever, yet gulls and swirling waders rose and fell. A heron cranked from distant scrape, cars a ribbon of red and white lights on the shadowed hill. Gradually light ebbed from this world, and it seemed possible to talk. But there was no need.

The sky was old, not us. The birds were archaic too. The water flows in and out, but the banks were broken and unrepaired. Ghosts here could talk, the winds freeze, the birds pick out our eyes, fish bite off fingers and toes. The mud took on a blue haze, electric beneath the aged sky that weighed so heavily.

Get out on the land. Let the brain forget to speak. The few starlings were a blur, and disappeared.

---

74. AN EAST WIND

It had been like this forever: a virus on the march, sending soon the shivers. A wind was roaring from the east, and we thought the seas could be interesting. Windscreen wipers snapped back and forth, but the rain blew away. On Frinton high street cars jostled for places, we waited for maneuvers to end. The greensward was empty, and we walked down the cliff path.

The North Sea was long and angry. Waves drove hard at the promenade, curling froth high and crashing down on beach and promenade and many-colored beach hut. The clouds raced gray and low. Dog walkers were out, but not one hut owner. All were sealed with rusted locks. Fishermen in oilskins headed for the point. A gap in the huts marked a social gradient, the end of Frinton and beginning of Walton. The tide rose, waders forced from the beach. Redshank picked at insects in algal scraps. Still the waves sucked back and charged forward.

Walton was locked in end-times, wishing for holiday seasons and getting only modern decay. Like other seaside towns, it lost to cheap overseas travel, had no answer. Save the economy, save the high street. There is hope, only if we consume more. But it has not worked here. The first building was crumbled, every window boarded, a peeling sign depicting luxury apartments never to be built. Red paint and hope had been slopped on a wall. Only pigeons huddled high on parapets. At the plastic pier of yellow and red, the main café was locked. In the distance was the beleaguered town and huts. The pier had an automated language. Lights on attractions blinked, sound loops called. *Ha ha ha,* laughed one. *Stand in a hurricane,* invited another. The dodgem cars were in a tired pile. An elderly fisherman hobbled slowly past, heading out to sea too. The wind outside battered the pier, waves sucking at the piles.

A sign to tenpin bowling, we pushed the door. At the alleys were family groups, resin balls thumping down the wooden lanes and sometimes crashing into pins. The cooks passed coffee and bacon rolls, and we sat above the water to look upon the distant land. We ate slowly. There was no hurry.

The bright pier advertising said, *There Is an Adventure Waiting for Everyone.* The wild, though, could save us. On the way back, the gale blew, more rain fell.

Thomas Merton wrote: "Everything is in fact paradise. This day will not come again."

We already have everything. Every year we change. A year of life is good; one hundred years of life is good too.

> The new year arrived
> In utter simplicity—
> And a deep blue sky.
>   Kobayashi Issa,
>   1763–1827

CROSSING THE NEW YEAR

Now here's a story I heard tell. It was a dusk and dawn like any other. Just a date in the diary. It was the New Year.

Every human culture celebrates the end of one annual cycle, the beginning of the next. We sing, drink, tell stories, give presents. We offer money to bring good fortune; we make sacrifices. World cities splash light on midnight skies, a fortune burned on fireworks.

As time passes,
Places change.
We chant;
Older and outworn,
All dust and closer to death.

We wonder: What does the future look like? And anyway, why should we worry? Some cultures have developed a sense that the passing of time must bring progress. The next year will bring innovation and improvements, greater wealth, better things. Others believe more in a greater circularity of time, where now, whenever that is, is best. Others still hope that post-death will bring paths to heavens rather than hell.

Animals and birds migrate each year, others are new or recent arrivals. Some are seen as good, others bad. The egret came and stayed, so did the crayfish. Pests and diseases come or grow in number, and all are bad. Some species have disappeared almost completely, the red squirrel and elm, others are on the rise, the otter and buzzard. The honeybee struggled for years and recovered slightly; some bumblebees thrive. The future will bring heightened threats, particularly if climate changes much.

There will be solutions too, people getting out more, being in nature, creating ceremonies and rituals that celebrate connections with both places and community. Aldo Leopold wrote in "The Land Ethic," "To sum up: a system of conservation based solely on economic self-interest is hopelessly lopsided." A new ethic will help us think of the economy as the environment.

Materialism has created dualisms: have and have-not. Yet we can appreciate something without having it: a view, birdsong, the perfume of flowers, the rustle of leaves, the laugh of children. The world has had enough. Go slower. There is a single white cloud in the sky. Sometime later, it is still there, and under the poplars rustle with the sound of a rushing river.

An old farm ethic from the east country states you should live as if tomorrow were your last, but farm the land as if you will live forever. Nature will survive us all. How it looks depends on our choices, our responsibilities. This is it, said Seamus Heaney. There is no next-time-round.

The New Year will be the same. The New Year will be different.

ACKNOWLEDGMENTS

I am very grateful to many people of the valley and shore, who have made observations and gave advice freely, particularly Ronald Blythe and John Rix in the valley, and those who narrated the land as they walked, including Rob Macfarlane, Chris Pretty, Ken Worpole, Brian and Toni Dawson. I am particularly grateful to the following for reading and commenting on earlier drafts of this almanac: Glenn Albrecht, Simon Amstutz, James Canton, Dave Charleston, Paul Ellis, Jenny Harpur, Kitty Liu, Susan Oliver, Gwen Roland, Julian Roughton, Ken Worpole. Others offered welcome encouragements: special thanks to Liz Calder, Jay Griffiths, Rachel Lichtenstein, Richard Mabey, Andy May. Three anonymous reviewers for Cornell University Press offered wise advice, and Kitty Liu steered the book to completion with a steady hand and wonderful insight. I am especially grateful to philosopher Glenn Albrecht for his vision on structure and form. Many other helpful observations on related or earlier work have been made on social media platforms: to all, many thanks.

NOTES BY TALE

PREFACE

The river Stour runs through the valley: some local people pronounce it *stower*, others *stir*. In 1705, an act of Parliament recorded it as the river Stower.

Screenwriter Jenny Harpur has called Seamus Heaney a "wholesome magician"; see the superb RTÉ documentary *Out of the Marvellous* (2009), directed by Charlie McCarthy. I am grateful to Ken Worpole for discovering and recommending D. W. Gillingham's remarkable *Unto the Fields* (1953). Paul Ellis talked of picking up a cold pebble and carrying it until warm.

JANUARY

1. See Ronald Blythe's *The Time by the Sea* (2013). John Masefield's quote is from the poem "Sea Fever" (in *Spunyarn*, 2011). Throughout this book, all temperatures are in degrees Celsius (°C) rather than Fahrenheit.

2. See Arthur Patterson's *Wildfowlers and Poachers* (1929), Robert Finch's *Outlands* (1986), Ambrose Waller's *The Suffolk Stour* (1959). In his *Out of Essex* (2013), James Canton discusses Sabine Baring-Gould, rector of Mersea; his famed book is *Mehalah* (1880). The shield duck is the old name for the piebald shellduck. Finch's *Outlands* is also an east country, journeys in the outer edges of Cape Cod. Historian John Norden's travelled through Essex in 1594; the quote is from Ronald Blythe's *In Praise of Essex* (1998).

3. At the time of the Conference of the Parties (COP21) in Paris, December 2015, atmospheric carbon was increasing at about two parts per million per year. Voluntary pledges of cuts in emissions were agreed, seeking to keep the temperature rise below 2° C above the preindustrial level, and aiming for 1.5° C.

4. The reference in the title is to Richard Long's ambulatory art, *Walking the Line* (2000). William Dutt describes the exit of the Ore in *Suffolk* (1909). There is a herd of Suffolk Punch horses at Hollesley Bay Prison (see J. Pretty, *This Luminous Coast*, 2011). The Johnny Cash lines are from his "I Walk the Line."

5. Seamus Heaney's comment is from the RTÉ documentary *Out of the Marvellous* (2009).

6. For an account of the Battle of Mealdune (Maldon), both the original and translated, see R. North, J. Allard, and J. Gillies, *Longman Anthology of Old English, Old Icelandic and Anglo-Norman Literature* (2011). After two hundred years of Viking raids and minor ruling, Cnut (or Canute) was the first to rule the whole of England. Popular lore says he was a fool to command the waves to retreat; accounts at the time indicate he set up the event to show his courtiers the value of humility: even a king could not command nature to do his bidding. The winner of the Danegeld from the Battle of Mealdune, Olaf, then brought Christianity to the Norse as king,

was made a saint, and now a pilgrimage way of 640 kilometers leads to his grave at the Nidaros Cathedral in Trondheim, Norway.

FEBRUARY

7. The phrase "blue remembered hills" is from A. E. Housman's 1896 poem, and later a Dennis Potter play. The Naitō Jōshō haiku is in J. Clements, *Zen Haiku* (2000).

8. The Matsuo Bashō haiku is in J. Clements, *Zen Haiku* (2000). It is also translated by June Reichhold (*Bashō: The Complete Haiku*, 2008) as:

> summer grass
> the only remains of soldiers'
> dreams.

See also in M. Bashō, *The Narrow Road to the Deep North* (1968):

> a thicket of grass
> Is all that remains
> Of dreams and ambitions
> Of ancient warriors.

10. The comment on skylark song is in Mark Cocker and Richard Mabey's *Birds Britannica* (2005). The Stour River is fed from the north by the underground Ely-Ouse water transfer, thus bringing water from Norfolk and the Fens to dry south Essex.

11. Philip Connors's book about fire lookouts is *Fire Season* (2011). The Open Road bookshop is run by Dave Charleston and can be found in Stoke-by-Nayland: https://theopenroadbookshop. wordpress.com/.

MARCH

12. The quote from Lama Anagarika Govinda is in *The Way of the White Cloud* (1966).

13. See Patrick Wright's *The River* (1999) for an account of the whole Thames River. For more on clever corvids, see J. Marzluff and T. Angell's *Gift of the Crow* (2012).

14. John Constable's altar painting in Nayland church is *Christ Blessing the Bread and Wine of the Last Supper*, commissioned in 1809 by the artist's aunt.

15. See Richard Mabey's *Flora Britannica* (1996) for more on *Prunus* species and cherries from Asia. I am grateful to Richard for an email on the common error about cherry plum and blackthorn in spring flower.

APRIL

17. Simon Amstutz of the Dedham Vale and Stour Valley Project notes that the Forestry Commission, led by Simon Leatherdale, helped the spread of buzzards by cutting the tops out of trees.

18. See Dōgen Zenji's *Moon in a Dewdrop* (trans. K. Tanahashi, 1985). For T. S. Eliot's *Four Quartets*, see Blamires, *Word Unheard* (1969).

19. The Matsuo Bashō haiku is in J. Clements, *Zen Haiku* (2000).

20. On the performance of nightingales, see Mark Cocker and Richard Mabey's *Birds Britannica* (2005) and Richard Mabey's *Book of Nightingales* (1997).

22. See S. L. Bensusan's *A Marshland Omnibus* (1954). The comment about elms is in Ronald Blythe's *Word from Wormingford* (1997).

MAY

23. The silt often deposited on cars is popularly assumed to have been transported from the Sahara Desert by southerly winds. It is known to be supplemented by dry deposits of ammonium nitrate, the nitrogen derived from exhausts of motor vehicles. The village efforts on solar photovoltaics and other renewables have been led by Will Hitchcock and Transition Nayland. The Matsuo Bashō haiku is in *Bashō: The Complete Haiku* (trans. J. Reichhold, 2008).

24. John Rix's farm enterprises (P. S. Rix Farms, Stourgarden) have an important influence on the valley. They farm 5,500 acres with twenty-six contract farming arrangements with other landlords and owners. "We farm as if we own the land," says Rix. The average field size is twenty-five acres. A total of 5 percent of land is not in production (pollen and nectar strips, wild bird covers, grass margins, field corners), with wildlife a key part of all operations. All of the farms are in national stewardship schemes. They have recently established a fifty-six-acre solar photovoltaic array with 76,000 panels, grazed by three hundred sheep. They grow potato, onion, sugar beet, winter barley, lettuce, winter wheat, and grass, each year producing some sixty thousand tons of produce. They run a herd of pedigree Charolais and South Devon suckler cows, grazing mainly 350 acres of river meadow and marginal lands. Irrigation is critical: they have built fourteen reservoirs, though still purchase licenses for river water extraction. They are active in public relations, ensuring footpaths are open and tractors pull over on roads, have built back paths and tracks to keep machinery out of villages, and planted hedgerows. Stourgarden is a packing and preparation operation to add value to produce from the valley, employing 140 staff, including mainly Nepali Gurkhas and young east Europeans. "We enjoy farming; we enjoy the vale," says Rix. Research at the Centre for Hydrology and Ecology has shown that removing 3 to 8 percent of agricultural land from production for wildlife habitats not only does not reduce crop yields (wheat, oilseed rape, legumes, grasses) but also often leads to increases (R. F. Pywell et al., "Wildlife-Friendly Farming," 2015).

25. The account of the Duke and Duchess of Norfolk's meals is in Ambrose Waller's *The Suffolk Stour* (1959). The Lao-tzu lines are from the *Tao Te-Ching* (S. Addis and S. Lombardo, *Lao-Tzu*, 1993).

26. In the early 1960s, the British Railways Board identified 2,363 stations and 5,000 miles of railway line for closure, 55% of stations and 30% of route miles. The recommendations came from reports by Richard Beeching and came to be known as the Beeching cuts.

27. The story of Rene Horwood's night of the floods in 1953 is in J. Pretty, *This Luminous Coast* (2011).

28. The new Essex Wildlife Trust reserve at Mucking is Thurrock Thameside Nature Park. Essex Wildlife Trust was led with distinction by John Hall for many years, a period in which it took on more than eighty-seven nature reserves, created wetlands and marsh, and built nine visitor centers. It has 35,000 members. The Matsuo Bashō haiku is in *The Penguin Book of Japanese Verse* (Bownas, 1964). It is also translated by June Reichhold (*Bashō: The Complete Haiku*, 2008) as:

Lightning flash
Flying towards the darkness
Heron's voice.

30. The local community at West Bergholt has been active in Hillhouse Wood to create a dramatic bluebell landscape: www.westbergholt.net/clubs/hillhouse-wood.

JUNE

31. For an account of Cunning Murrell's life, see A. Morrison, *Cunning Murrell* (1900).

32. For the Edward FitzGerald quote, see W. G. Arnott, *Alde Estuary* (1973). "Sun burnt tar that blisters on the planks" is from George Crabbe's *Borough* (1810).

33. See Richard Jefferies's *Wild Life in a Southern County* (2011 [1879]) for the use of "humble-bee." D. W. Gillingham wrote of red squirrel in *Unto the Fields* (1953). The Li Po poem excerpt is from S. Hamill and J. P. Seaton, *The Poetry of Zen* (2007).

34. On window strikes: Glenn Albrecht has described the daily observation of regent bower-birds on his farm in Australia, and the dismay of discovering the female dead by the veranda windows one morning. He rescued the chicks high up in their stick nest; one survived and was released. See "Antipodean Nature Notes" on Facebook (2015).

35. The Matsuo Bashō haiku is in J. Clements, *Zen Haiku* (2000, 64). In Bashō, *The Narrow Road to the Deep North* (1968), it is translated as:

Tired of walking
I put up at an inn
Embraced comfortably
By wisteria flowers.

37. For lost medieval villages, see M. W. Beresford, *The Lost Villages of England* (1954), and M. W. Beresford and J. Hurst, *Deserted Medieval Villages* (1979). Christopher Woodward's commentary on Rome and the Colosseum is in his *In Ruins* (2002). The comment on Deakin's research is also contained in *In Ruins*.

JULY

39. On edgelands, see Paul Farley and Michael Roberts's *Edgelands* (2011).

40. On the visibility of the power station mentioned by Sebald in *The Rings of Saturn*: BBC tele-vision's *Springwatch* broadcast from Minsmere for several years, and camera angles never seemed to spot the power station. The sand dunes at Sizewell are artificial: they are part of the sea defenses for the power station. I have written of the wild returning to the Chernobyl exclusion zone in the three decades since the disastrous fire in 1986: see J. Pretty. *The Earth Only Endures* (2007).

41. On allotments, see D. Crouch and C. Ward's *The Allotment* (1974). Little Lye is owned by Andora Carver in Nayland village.

42. Cash evokes the tone and content of the original "The Wanderer" poem, composed in Anglo-Saxon and sourced from the *Exeter Book*. The poem dates from the ninth century. The lyrics of both Ernie Maresca (for Dion in 1961) and Bono (for Johnny Cash in 1993) contain many echoes of the anonymous poem (see North, Allard, and Gillies, eds., *Longman Anthology of Old English, Old Icelandic and Anglo-Norman Literatures*, 2011).

AUGUST

44. John Clare's lines on ragwort can be found in his 1832 poem "The Ragwort."

45. For an account of walking Halvergate with Billy Frosdick, see J. Pretty, *The Edge of Extinction* (2014). For a haunting account of east coast habitats, see Julian Tennyson's *Suffolk Scene* (1939). See also J. Wentworth-Day's *Marshland Adventure* (1950). For early maps of the Suffolk coast, see D. Dymond's *John Kirby's Suffolk* (2004). George Crabbe wrote of the coast in his poem, *The Borough* (1810). In the preface, Crabbe denied he had any particular place in mind, but it clearly owed much to Aldeburgh.

48. For an account of the Suffolk railway, see W. G. Sebald's *Rings of Saturn* (2002), and J. Pretty's *This Luminous Coast* (2011, 194–95). Terns were long known as sea swallows.

SEPTEMBER

50. Here football is soccer, and the team is Colchester United. On horses, see Thomas Hardy's "In Time of 'The Breaking of Nations'": "Only a man harrowing clods / In a slow silent walk / With an old horse that stumbles and nods / Half asleep as they stalk / . . . Yet this will go onward the same / Though Dynasties pass."

51. Both Samuel Bensusan's *A Marshland Omnibus* (1954) and J. A. Baker's *The Peregrine* (1967) were set on the Dengie Peninsula, flanked by the rivers Blackwater and Crouch and the North Sea. John Betjeman's poem about Essex is in I. Gould and B. M. Gould's *An Anthology of Essex* (1911). The Wentworth-Day story is in his *Marshland Adventure* (1950).

52. For travels by horse and coach in Suffolk, see Daniel Defoe's *A Tour through the Whole Island of Great Britain* (1724–1726) and François de La Rochefoucauld's *A Frenchman's Year in Suffolk* (1784). The cyclist was Mark Cavendish, second-highest winner of stages in the Tour de France (as of 2016).

55. For accounts of twentieth-century farm life in Suffolk, see George Ewart Evans's *Ask the Fellow Who Cut the Hay* (1955), *The Horse and the Furrow* (1960), and *The Pattern under the Plough* (1966); Ronald Blythe's *Akenfield* (1969); Adrian Bell's *Corduroy* (1930) and *Apple Acre* (1942); and Hugh Barrett's *Early to Rise* (1967). The Annie Dillard quote is from *Teaching a Stone to Talk* (1982).

OCTOBER

57. The quote from Seamus Heaney is in the RTÉ Television documentary, *Out of the Marvellous* (2009).

58. For "Doubt is our product," see N. Oreskes and E. M. Conway, *Merchants of Doubt* (2010). Shelley's quote is from his poem "To a Skylark." The Lao-tzu lines are from the *Tao Te-Ching* (S. Addis and S. Lombardo, *Lao-Tzu*, 1993).

59. T. S. Eliot's bird cries in *The Four Quartets* (see H. Blamires, *Word Unheard* 1969).

60. The quote from Seamus Heaney is in the RTÉ Television documentary, *Out of the Marvellous* (2009). For the earlier account of walking on the Broomway on the Maplin Sands off the Essex coast, see J. Pretty, *This Luminous Coast* (2011).

NOVEMBER

62. Guy Fawkes night is celebrated with large bonfires and fireworks on the 5th of November in the UK. He was a member of a group of Catholics who attempted to bomb the Houses of Parliament in 1605. The failure has been commemorated since 1605.

63. Mrs. Paine of Pier Avenue, Southwold, was a friend of my grandmother and bred a pure scarlet geranium; Cedric Morris's pale pink was passed to Ronnie Blythe and a cutting to me. Both live on.

64. The excerpt is from Dylan Thomas's "Do not go gentle into that good night." The Thomas Hardy letter is quoted in Geoffrey Mann's *Southwold: An Earthly Paradise* (2006).

65. Colette Bailey runs Metal Culture in Chalkwell, Southend; see http://www.metal culture.com/.

66. On the naming of storms: the meteorological offices of Britain and Ireland began naming North Atlantic storms in late 2015, beginning with Abigail, Barney, Clodagh, Desmond, Eva, Frank, Gertrude, Henry, Imogen, Jake, and Katie (arriving in late March 2016). The Norfolk coastal town of Happisburgh is pronounced Haisboro.

DECEMBER

69. The quote from Peter Avery is in J. Pretty, *This Luminous Coast* (2011).

70. "Poor Man's Heaven" is sung by Tom Goddard on *Good Order! Traditional Music from The Eel's Foot* (2000). S. L. Bensusan comments about the country in his *Salt of the Marshes* (1949).

73. The comment about grim Bulcamp Workhouse is from Ronald Blythe's *The View in Winter* (1979).

74. The Thomas Merton quote is in Douglas Christie's *Blue Sapphire of the Mind* (2013). Kobayashi Issa's haiku is in Sam Hamill's *The Sound of Water* (1995).

BIBLIOGRAPHY

Abbey, E. 1968. *Desert Solitaire*. New York: Simon and Schuster.

Addis, S., and S. Lombardo, trans. 1993. *Lao-Tzu: Tao Te-Ching*. Indianapolis: Hackelt.

Anderson, E. 1996. *Ecologies of the Heart*. New York: Oxford University Press.

Arnott, W. G. 1973. *Alde Estuary*. Ipswich: Boydell Press.

Baker, J. A. 1967 [2005]. *The Peregrine*. New York: New York Review Books.

——. 1969. *The Hill of Summer*. London: Collins.

Baring-Gould, S. 1880 [1998]. *Mehalah*. London: Praxis.

Barrett, H. 1967. *Early to Rise*. London: Faber and Faber.

Bashō, M. 1968. *The Narrow Road to the Deep North and Other Travel Sketches*. Translated by N. Yuasa. London: Penguin.

——. 2008. *Bashō: The Complete Haiku*. Translated by J. Reichhold. Tokyo: Kodansha International.

Bell, A. 1930 [2000]. *Corduroy*. London: Penguin.

——. 1942 [2012]. *Apple Acre*. Dorchester, Dorset: Little Toller Press.

Benham, H. 1971. *Once Upon a Tide*. London: Harrap.

Bensusan, S. L. 1949. *Salt of the Marshes*. London: Routledge and Kegan Paul.

——. 1954. *A Marshland Omnibus*. London: Duckworth.

Beresford, M. W. 1954. *The Lost Villages of England*. London: Lutterworth Press.

Beresford, M. W., and J. Hurst. 1979. *Deserted Medieval Villages*. New York: St. Martin's Press.

Blamires, H. 1969. *Word Unheard: A Guide through Eliot's* Four Quartets. London: Methuen.

Blythe, R. 1969. *Akenfield*. London: Penguin.

——. 1979 [2005]. *The View in Winter*. Norwich: Canterbury Press.

——. 1988. *In Praise of Essex: An Anthology*. Bury St Edmunds: Alastair Press.

——. 1997. *Word from Wormingford*. London: Penguin.

——. 2006. *A Year at Bottengoms Farm*. Norwich: Canterbury Press.

——. 2008. *Outsiders*. Norwich: Canterbury Press.

——. 2008. *River Diary*. Norwich: Canterbury Press.

——. 2011. *At the Yeoman's House*. London: Enitharmon Press.

——. 2013. *The Time by the Sea*. London: Faber and Faber.

Bownas, G. 1964 [1998]. *The Penguin Book of Japanese Verse*. London: Penguin.

Butcher, D. 1979. *The Driftermen*. Reading: Tops'l Books.

——. 1982. *Living from the Sea*. Reading: Tops'l Books.

Camus, A. 1942. *L'Étranger*. London: Penguin.

Canton, J. 2013. *Out of Essex. Re-Imagining a History of Landscape*. Oxford: Signal Books.

Cash, J. 2005. *Ring of Fire: The Legend of Johnny Cash*. CD. London: Island.

Christie, D. 2013. *Blue Sapphire of the Mind*. Oxford: Oxford University Press.

Clegg, R., and S. Clegg. 1999. *Southwold*. Chichester: Phillimore.

Clements, J. 2000. *Zen Haiku*. London: Francis Lincoln.

Cocker, M. 2007. *Crow Country*. London: Jonathan Cape.

——. 2014. *Claxton: Field Notes from a Small Planet*. London: Jonathan Cape.

Cocker, M., and R. Mabey. 2005. *Birds Britannica*. London: Chatto and Windus.

Collins, J. S. 2011. *The Wood*. London: Penguin.

Connors, P. 2011. *Fire Season*. London: Macmillan.

Crossley, A., M. Dunn, and F. Heard. 2000. *Tollesbury in the Year 2000*. Tollesbury: Tollesbury Millennium Publishing.

Crouch, D., and C. Ward. 1997. *The Allotment*. Nottingham: Five Leaves.

Davies, D. J. 2005. *A Brief History of Death*. Oxford: Blackwell.

Deakin, R. 2000. *Waterlog*. London: Vintage.

——. 2007. *Wildwood: A Journey through Trees*. London: Hamish Hamilton.

Defoe, D. 1724–1726 [1972]. *A Tour through the Whole Island of Great Britain*. London: Penguin.

Dillard, A. 1982. *Teaching a Stone to Talk*. New York: Harper Perennial.

——. 1990. *Pilgrim at Tinker Creek*. In *Three by Annie Dillard*, 1–260. 2001. New York: Harper Perennial.

Dōgen Zenji. 1985. *Moon in a Dewdrop*. Edited by K. Tanahashi. New York: North Point Press.

Dutt, W. A. 1904. *Highways and Byways in East Anglia*. London: Macmillan.

——. 1909. *Suffolk*. Cambridge: Cambridge University Press.

Dymond, D., ed. 2004. *John Kirby's Suffolk: His Maps and Roadbooks*. Woodbridge: Boydell Press.

Evans, G. E. 1955. *Ask the Fellows Who Cut the Hay*. London: Faber and Faber.

——. 1960. *The Horse and the Furrow*. London: Faber and Faber.

——. 1966. *The Pattern under the Plough*. London: Faber and Faber.

Farley, P., and M. S. Roberts. 2011. *Edgelands*. London: Jonathan Cape.

Finch, R. 1986. *Outlands: Journeys to the Outer Edge of Cape Cod*. Boston: David Godine.

Gillingham, D. W. 1953. *Unto the Fields*. London: Country Book Club.

Good Order! Songs from The Eel's Foot. 2000. CD. London: BBC.

Gould, I., and B. M. Gould. 1911. *An Anthology of Essex*. London: Samson Low Marston and Co.

Govinda, Lama A. 1966 [2006]. *The Way of the White Cloud*. London: Rider.

Grieve, H. 1959. *The Great Tide*. Chelmsford: Essex County Council.

Griffiths, J. 2006. *Wild: An Elemental Journey*. London: Hamish Hamilton.

Haggard, L. R. 1935 [1982]. *I Walked by Night: By the King of the Norfolk Poachers*. Oxford: Oxford University Press.

Hambling, M. 2012. *The Scallop*. Saxmundham: Full Circle Editions.

Hamill, S. 1995. *The Sound of Water*. Boston: Shambhala.

Hamill, S., and J. P. Seaton, trans. and eds. 2007. *The Poets of Zen*. Boston: Shambhala.

Hanbury-Tenison, R. 2006. *The Seventy Great Journeys*. London: Thames and Hudson.

Heaney, S. 1999. *Beowulf*. London: Faber and Faber.

——. 2002. *Finders Keepers*. London: Faber and Faber.

Heaton, A. 2001. *Duck Decoys*. Princes Risborough, Bucks.: Shire Books.

Hinton, D., trans and ed. 2002. *Mountain Home: The Wilderness Poetry of Ancient China*. London: Anvil Press Poetry.

Jefferies, R. 2011 [1879]. *Wild Life in a Southern County*. Dorchester, Dorset: Little Toller.

Johnson, D. E. 1992. *East Anglia at War, 1939–1945*. Norwich: Jarold.

Kunitz, S. 2005. *The Wild Braid*. New York: W. W. Norton and Co.

Larkin P. 2003. *Collected Poems*. London: Faber and Faber.

La Rochefoucauld, F. de. 1988. *A Frenchman's Year in Suffolk, 1784*. Translated by N. Scarfe. Woodbridge: Boydell Press.

Leather, J. 1979. *The Salty Shore*. Lavenham: Terrence Dalton.

Leopold, A. 1949 [1974]. *A Sand County Almanac and Sketches Here and There*. New York: Oxford University Press.

Long, R. 2002. *Walking the Line*. London: Thames and Hudson.

Lopez, B. 1988. *Crossing Open Ground*. London: Picador.

——. 1998. *About This Life*. London: Harvill.

Mabey, R. 1996. *Flora Britannica*. London: Sinclair-Stevenson.

——. 1997. *The Book of Nightingales*. London: Sinclair-Stevenson.

——. 2007. *Beechcombings*. London: Chatto and Windus.

——. 2015. *The Cabaret of Plants: Botany and the Imagination*. London: Profile.

Macfarlane, R. 2007. *The Wild Places*. London: Granta.

——. 2012. *The Old Ways*. London: Hamish Hamilton.

——. 2014. *Landmarks*. London: Hamish Hamilton.

Mann G. 2006. *Southwold: An Earthly Paradise*. Woodbridge: ACC Art Books.

Marzluff, J., and T. Angell. 2012. *Gift of the Crow*. New York: Free Press.

Masefield, J. 2011. *Spunyarn: Sea Poetry and Prose*. London: Penguin.

McCarthy, C., dir. 2009. *Out of the Marvellous*. DVD. Dublin: RTÉ Television.

Morrison, A. 1900. *Cunning Murrell*. New York: Doubleday, Page and Co.

North, R., J. Allard, and P. Gillies, eds. 2011. *Longman Anthology of Old English, Old Icelandic and Anglo-Norman Literatures*. London: Longman.

O'Driscoll, D. 2009. *Stepping Stones: Interviews with Seamus Heaney*. London: Faber and Faber.

Oreskes, N., and E. M. Conway. 2010. *Merchants of Doubt*. New York: Bloomsbury.

Orton J., and Worpole K. 2005. *350 Miles. An Essex Journey*. Chelmsford: Essex Development and Regeneration Agency.

Patterson, A. H. 1929 [1988]. *Wildfowlers and Poachers*. Southampton: Ashford Press.

Pretty, J. 2002. *Agri-Culture*. London: Earthscan.

——. 2007. *The Earth Only Endures*. London: Earthscan.

——. 2011. *This Luminous Coast*. Saxmundham: Full Circle Editions. Cloth ed.: 2014. Ithaca: Cornell University Press.

——. 2014. *The Edge of Extinction*. Ithaca: Cornell University Press.

Pywell, R. F., M. S. Heard, B. A. Woodcock, S. Hinsley, L. Ridding, M. Nowakowski, and J. M. Bullock. 2015. "Wildlife-Friendly Farming Increases Crop Yield: Evidence for Ecological Intensification." *Proceedings of Royal Society of London B* 240, 1740.

Richens, R. H. 1983. *Elm*. Cambridge: Cambridge University Press.

Scarfe, N. 1960. *Essex*. London: Faber and Faber.

——. 1960. *Suffolk*. London: Faber and Faber.

Sebald, W. G. 2002. *The Rings of Saturn*. London: Vintage.

Stegner, W. 1962. *Wolf Willow*. London: Penguin.

Street, A. G. 1932. *Farmer's Glory*. London: Faber and Faber.

Tanahashi, K., ed. 1985. *Moon in a Dewdrop: Writings of Zen Master Dogen*. New York: North Point Press.

Tennyson, J. 1939. *Suffolk Scene. A Book of Description and Adventure*. London: Blackie and Son.

Tompkins, H. 1904. *Marsh Country Rambles*. London: Chatto and Windus.

Turner, J. 1996. *The Abstract Wild*. Tucson: University of Arizona Press.

Uttley, A. 1952. *Ploughman's Clocks*. London: Faber and Faber.

Walker, S. 2011. *The Spirit of Design*. London: Earthscan.

Waller, A. J. R. 1959. *The Suffolk Stour*. Ipswich: Norman Alard.

Wentworth Day, J. 1949. *Coastal Adventure*. London: Harrap.

——. 1950. *Marshland Adventure*. London: Harrap.

——. 1956. *They Walk the Wild Places*. London: Blandford Press.

Westwood, J., and J. Simpson. 2005. *The Lore of the Land*. London: Penguin.

Woodward, C. 2002. *In Ruins*. London: Vintage.

Wright, P. 1999. *The River: The Thames in Our Time*. London: BBC.

Young, A. 1813 [1969]. *General View of the Agriculture of the County of Suffolk*. Plymouth: David and Charles.

PHOTOGRAPHS

CPSIA information can be obtained
at www.ICGtesting.com
Printed in the USA
LVOW03s2039260917
550142LV00004B/365/P